PELICAN BOOKS
A469

UNDERSTANDING WEATHER

O. G. SUTTON

Sir Graham Sutton is Director-General of the Meteorological Office. He is a native of Monmouthshire and,
appropriately, of Welsh and English extraction. He was
educated at Pontywaun Grammar School, the University College of Wales, Aberystwyth, and Jesus College,
Oxford (of which he is now an Honorary Fellow). He
has spent most of his life in Government scientific
establishments, working mainly in micrometeorology.
During the war, however, he was in charge of research
in chemical defence and, later, in tank armaments. In
1945 he was made Chief Superintendent of the Radar
Research and Development Establishment at Malvern.
From there he went to the Royal Military College of
Science, Shrivenham, where he was both Professor of
Mathematical Physics and Dean. He was elected a
Fellow of the Royal Society in 1949, and was knighted
in 1955.

His wife was a fellow student at Aberystwyth and
they have two sons. He lives at Sunninghill, near Ascot,
and is a Justice of the Peace for Berkshire.

O. G. SUTTON

UNDERSTANDING WEATHER

PENGUIN BOOKS

Penguin Books Ltd, Harmondsworth, Middlesex, England
Penguin Books Inc., 3300 Clipper Mill Road, Baltimore 11, Md, u.s.a.
Penguin Books Pty Ltd, Ringwood,
Victoria, Australia

—

First published 1960
Reprinted 1961
Second Edition 1964

—

—

Made and printed in Great Britain
by C. Nicholls & Company Ltd
Gravure plates by Harrison
Set in Monotype Baskerville

Contents

List of Plates

List of Figures

Preface

THIS book is a series of essays on some aspects of weather which I believe are of interest to the general reader. It makes no claim to be a systematic account of meteorology, and in a sense is a progress report on the science of the atmosphere. As such I hope it will help towards a better understanding, not only of weather, but also of the way in which the meteorologist approaches his problems.

Some parts of the book were read in manuscript by my colleagues, Dr J. M. Stagg, Dr R. C. Sutcliffe, Dr A. C. Best, and Mr D. M. Houghton, whose help I gratefully acknowledge. I am also indebted to Mr G. A. Bull, the Librarian of the Meteorological Office, for assistance in selecting photographs, and to my wife for her aid in the preparation and proof reading of the text.

O. G. SUTTON

Sunninghill, Berks
December 1959

Preface to the Second Edition

THIS edition contains some additional information on the use of rockets and artificial satellites for meteorological purposes. I have also taken the opportunity to revise Chapter 7, on long-range forecasts, and to add an appendix on scales of temperature in the light of recent events.

It is a pleasure to acknowledge the help given to me in this revision by Professor W. van der Bijl of the University of Kansas and by Mr A. Gilchrist of the Meteorological Office.

O. G. SUTTON

Sunninghill, Berks
September 1963

CHAPTER I

The Atmosphere of the Earth

WHEN compared with the radius of the earth (about 4,000 miles) the atmosphere appears as a thin skin of gas which is prevented from escaping into space by the force of gravity. On this scale, we live at the bottom of a very shallow ocean of air which has no definite upper surface. The extreme fringe of the atmosphere is conventionally supposed to be about 1,000 kilometres (600 miles) above sea level, but this statement does not bring out the extremely rarefied state of the gases which exist at such heights. Even at 100 kilometres (60 miles) the density of the air is only one-millionth of that at the ground, and above 300 kilometres (200 miles) pressure is lower than that which can be produced in a laboratory by a vacuum pump.

Meteorology, as a science and as a profession, is primarily concerned with processes in the main mass of the earth's atmosphere. It is worth recalling in these days of high-flying aircraft and artificial satellites that about five-sixths of the total mass of the atmosphere, and by far the greater part of its moisture content, lie inside a layer which, in the middle latitudes, is not more than seven or eight miles deep.

Clean dry air is a mixture of gases, chiefly nitrogen (78 per cent), oxygen (21 per cent), argon (less than 1 per cent), and carbon dioxide (about 0·03 per cent), together with very small amounts of the so-called 'rare' gases. The atmosphere in which we live contains, in addition, variable amounts of water and pollution, chiefly smoke and dust. As far as the two principal gases are concerned, the evidence indicates that the proportions found at the surface are maintained unchanged up to heights of at least 70 kilometres (40 miles).

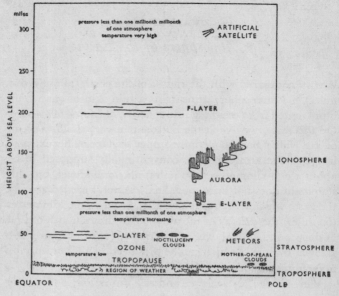

Fig. 1 – The structure of the earth's atmosphere

Fig. 1 is a picture of the broad structure of the atmosphere up to about 500 kilometres (300 miles). The 'weather', which plays so large a part in our daily lives is confined, for the most part, to the lowest layer, known as the *troposphere*. Above this lies the *stratosphere*, a region of thin, almost cloudless air, which we may suppose to extend to about 80 kilometres (50 miles). The present interests of meteorology largely cease at this level, above which lies the *ionosphere*, characterized by electrically conducting layers which make long-distance radio transmission possible by reflecting electromagnetic waves back to earth. In the lower regions of the ionosphere the aurora brings beauty to the night sky in high latitudes.

The primary purpose of meteorology is to explain, and if

possible to predict, the behaviour of the atmosphere by the study of its physical properties. Air is a fluid, that is, an aggregation of molecules in incessant motion. The atmosphere has mass and can be weighed by measuring its pressure. The energy of molecular motion is manifest as heat, and is measured as temperature. In addition to its molecular motion, which is always present, the air sometimes moves in bulk, and this motion is measured as wind. The energy required to initiate and sustain such motion is derived entirely from the sun, so that the meteorologist must pay a great deal of attention to radiation. Finally, the atmosphere contains water, as a gas (water vapour) or in suspension as a liquid (clouds and rain) or a solid (clouds, snow, and hail). Water is not only the most variable, but also, to the meteorologist, by far the most important constituent of air. It is chiefly because of the water content of the atmosphere that meteorology is the most difficult of all branches of physical science. If we lived in an entirely dry atmosphere (supposing this to be possible with some form of intelligent life) there would be no weather and, presumably, no meteorologists, and throughout this book we shall have much to say about the role of water in the physical processes of the atmosphere.

STATICS OF THE ATMOSPHERE

In building up the analytical science of meteorology (as distinct from the mere collection and processing of observations) we must be prepared to consider first some ideal situations, from which we can progress to more realistic and complicated studies. In other words, to explain what is observed, we first construct in our minds 'model atmospheres', analyse them mathematically, and compare the results with observations made in the real atmosphere. The simplest possible model is that of a stagnant ocean of air resting on a flat uniform earth and extending indefinitely upwards. Such a model requires only the simplest mathematics for its analysis, and yet, as we shall see, is capable of yielding results which are by no means trivial.

In dealing with fluids, mass is most conveniently expressed by *density*, or mass per unit volume. The density of air at sea level fluctuates, but is never very far removed from about 1,200 grams per cubic metre. The density of a gas is related to its temperature and pressure by what is called the *equation of state* which, in its simplest form, says that density is proportional to the quotient of pressure and temperature. The *pressure* of the atmosphere, the quantity measured by the barometer, is simply the weight of a column of air, of unit cross-section, lying above the place of observation. This fact, written in the language of the calculus, constitutes the *hydrostatic equation*, the basic relation between density, pressure, gravity, and height in our model atmosphere.

Density is difficult to measure directly, so the equation of state is used to replace it in the hydrostatic equation by pressure and temperature. The hydrostatic equation can then be solved to give the *barometer-height formula*, which relates pressure to temperature and height. If we know precisely how temperature changes with height, we can then calculate the pressure at any height in our ideal atmosphere. But usually we do not know this, so as a first step we simplify the model still further by postulating that the atmosphere has the same temperature throughout (or, what is the same thing, we replace the real variable temperature by its average value), and for this *isothermal atmosphere* we find the simple relation

$$p_z = p_o e^{-gz/RT_m}$$

where p_z is the pressure at height z, p_o is the surface pressure, T_m is the average temperature and g and R are the acceleration due to gravity and the gas constant (the factor of proportionality in the equation of state) respectively. Thus in an ideal isothermal atmosphere the relation between pressure and height follows a smooth exponential curve, starting with a definite value at the surface and decreasing towards zero as the height increases indefinitely.

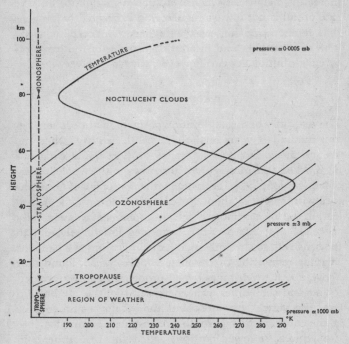

Fig. 2 – Temperature in the high atmosphere

Despite the omission of many important features of the real atmosphere, this simple theoretical relation compares well with reality as far as pressure is concerned and, in a slightly more sophisticated form, is the basis of the usual type of aircraft altimeter. The observed decrease of pressure with height is sufficiently regular to allow the equation to be inverted and used to determine height from measurements of pressure. It is otherwise with temperature, which could not be used to determine height with any confidence. It is a commonplace experience that temperature falls with increasing height, as when we climb a mountain, but the rate of fall is not always regular and it frequently happens that temperature increases with height in certain layers. The most striking and interesting features of the temperature distribution appear, however, when we go very high.

THE STRATOSPHERE

The real story of the exploration of the high atmosphere begins in the last years of the nineteenth century, when the French meteorologist Teisserence de Bort made what has been called 'the most striking discovery in the whole history of meteorology'. On the average, the rate of fall of temperature with height is about 0·6°c. in 100 metres (1°F. in 300 feet) in the lower regions of the atmosphere. It was generally supposed that this decrease continued indefinitely, out to the fringe of the atmosphere, but de Bort, using free balloons carrying registering thermometers (*ballonsondes*), found that above about seven miles over Europe, temperature ceased to fall and sometimes even increased slightly. He had, in fact, discovered the stratosphere, and it is now commonplace in meteorology to regard the atmosphere as divided into two regions, a lower portion, called the troposphere, in which temperature decreases with height, and an upper portion, where it does not, but this simple view of the stratosphere has to be modified when very great heights are considered.

The surface of separation of the stratosphere and the troposphere, which for most purposes marks the upper limit of the phenomena of weather, is called the *tropopause*. The tropopause slopes from the equator to the poles, being about eleven miles above the tropical regions and five miles over the poles, which means that the coldest part of the stratosphere, and therefore of the whole atmosphere, lies over the hottest part of the earth.

The reason for this unexpected division of the atmosphere was first given by the British meteorologist Ernest Gold in a mathematical paper published in 1909. The full theory is too mathematical to be reproduced here except in outline. We need first to recall that heat can be transported from one place to another in three distinct ways: by radiation, by conduction, and by convection. Radiation consists of electromagnetic waves like those of radio, and enables heat to cross the almost empty space between the sun and the fringe of the atmosphere. Conduction of heat is brought about by collisions between molecules, and air is generally classed as a bad conductor. Convection means the spread of heat by the mixing of large masses of air, either because the heated masses move upwards as a result of their reduced density (buoyant or natural convection) or because a wind brings hot and cold air together and thus causes mixing on a very large scale (forced convection). All three processes operate in the atmosphere, but convection is far more efficient than conduction in spreading heat.

The atmosphere derives all its heat from the sun, but indirectly. Radiation from the sun is mainly composed of short waves, and air has little power to absorb these. The direct effect of the sunbeams is chiefly to heat the earth, and the lower atmosphere receives most of its heat from the surface on which it rests, partly in the form of long-wave (infrared) radiation, partly by conduction, but chiefly by convection. It is therefore natural to expect convection to be the dominant process in the maintenance of the heat balance of the lower atmosphere, and radiation at the higher levels.

These considerations furnish the essential clues to the

problem of the stratosphere. On the whole, the average temperature of the earth is not changing, so that there must be an exact balance between incoming and outgoing heat. The lower layers must therefore approximate to a state of convective equilibrium, and the mathematical analysis of such an ideal atmosphere shows that it would have a definite upper boundary with a steady drop of temperature from the surface upwards at the rate of nearly 1°C. in 100 metres (about 0·6°F. in 100 feet). The observed rate of fall of temperature up to the tropopause is about two-thirds of this, so that the real atmosphere is not in perfect convective equilibrium, but we can say with certainty that the upward decrease of temperature characteristic of the troposphere arises as a result of the continuous mixing of air from different levels. The upwards decrease is accounted for, broadly, by the cooling of air as it expands on rising to levels of lower pressure and the heating of air that is forced down and compressed, but the whole process is complicated by the presence of water which is always being condensed from vapour, or evaporated, with a consequent release or absorption of heat.

It is impossible, of course, for an unconfined gas like the atmosphere to have a definite upper boundary, that is, to cease suddenly with a vacuum above, but we may take the top of the ideal convective atmosphere to represent the tropopause. Above this there must be a rarefied atmosphere in which convection plays no part. Radiation and conduction will be the decisive factors in this region, which will have no definite top and must tend to be of uniform temperature. This region we may identify with the stratosphere, at least in its lower parts.

There can be little doubt that this explanation of the two-layer structure of the atmosphere is basically correct, but the theory of the radiative equilibrium of the stratosphere is still incomplete. Some mixing does occur in the stratosphere, mainly as a result of the strong winds that can blow at these levels; this is shown by the uniformity of the composition of the atmosphere up to very great heights. The outstanding feature of the lower stratosphere, however, is its extreme dryness. The low temperatures at these heights means that there can be only very little water-vapour present at any time, and it is a matter of importance for theoretical meteorology to know if this amount is the maximum possible, that is, if the water-vapour present is saturated or not. Despite the great difficulties of making measurements of extremely small amounts of water at very low temperatures, the British meteorologists G. M. B. Dobson and A. W. Brewer have shown definitely that stratospheric air over England is exceedingly dry, so much so that it must have come from the equatorial stratosphere, a fact which has implications for the large-scale circulation of the atmosphere.

Above the tropopause, temperature does not change greatly with height until 20 kilometres (12 miles) is reached, when it starts to rise, reaching a maximum at about 50 kilometres (30 miles). Here the very thin air is about as warm as it is in summer in the British Isles. The existence of such a hot layer was first suspected from observations on meteors, and because the sounds of gunfire have often been heard at very great distances from battlefields, indicating a downward bending of the sound waves at great heights. The physical reason for the high temperature is the absorption of very short-wave (ultra-violet) radiation from the sun by ozone, which reaches a maximum concentration between 20 and 40 kilometres (12 and 25 miles).

Between 50 and 80 kilometres, temperature falls to a low level. This second minimum may be regarded as marking the limit of interest of present day meteorology. In this region noctilucent (night-luminous) clouds are occasionally seen after sunset; it is not known with certainty whether they are formed of ice crystals or dust. Above the level of the noctilucent clouds lies the ionosphere, in which the evidence points to a further rise in temperature, but at such heights the atmosphere is more a collection of isolated molecules and atoms than a fluid, and the usual concepts of the state of a gas must be used with caution.

EXPLORING THE HIGH ATMOSPHERE

Balloons

Meteorologists have long used balloons to gain information about regions of the atmosphere inaccessible to direct observation. The latest device, the *radio-sonde,* * is capable of transmitting back to earth details of pressure, temperature, and humidity at all levels up to 25 to 30 kilometres (16 to 20 miles). The greatest height reached by sounding balloons is about 40 kilometres (25 miles) and this is near the theoretical ceiling of buoyant devices. For information about the state of the atmosphere at higher levels it is necessary to employ indirect methods or to use rockets. We shall now consider some of these methods.

Sound Waves

Much of our knowledge of temperatures and winds at the higher levels comes from the study of the 'anomalous' propagation of sound. A sound wave is a ripple of pressure and its speed of travel depends, *inter alia,* upon the temperature of the medium through which it is passing. Refraction, or change in the direction of travel, is evidence of a change of speed of propagation in the medium. Most sounds become inaudible at a relatively short distance from their place of origin, but it has been known for a long time that the noise of gunfire or of explosions can often be heard not only in the region immediately around the source, but also in an outer

* See Appendix, p. 221.

zone distant 100 kilometres (60 miles) or more, with a 'zone of silence' between. Those in the inner zone receive sound waves which have travelled through the lower atmosphere, but the existence of the outer anomalous zone of audibility can be explained only by the hypothesis that the waves which reach the ground at this distance must have been refracted, or bent downwards, by the atmosphere at heights between 40 and 60 kilometres (25 and 37 miles). By the use of a network of special microphones designed to pick up

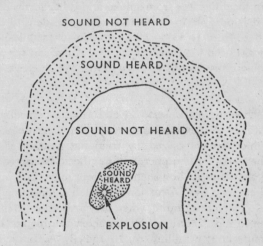

SOUND NOT HEARD

SOUND HEARD

SOUND NOT HEARD

SOUND HEARD

EXPLOSION

Fig. 3 – Anomalous propagation of sound waves

feeble sounds of low frequency, the time taken by the waves to travel from the site of a prearranged explosion, and their angle of descent, can be measured. From these data the temperature of the refracting layer can be estimated with fair consistency by the use of somewhat elaborate mathematical analysis. A pioneer in this investigation was the English meteorologist F. J. W. Whipple, who suggested, in 1935, that there must be a hot layer on the high atmosphere, together with a monsoon system of winds, easterly in summer and westerly in winter. Since that time, Whipple's conjectures have been amply confirmed.

Searchlights

The high atmosphere is almost free from dust, and the light from the upper part of the beam of a powerful search-light directed vertically is scattered mainly by air molecules. By measuring the intensity of this scattered light on a clear night, in localities free from smoke and other forms of pollution, it is possible to deduce values of the density of the atmosphere from 10 to 70 kilometres (6 to 45 miles). The method has been used with success by American scientists, and is now in use in this country on the Welsh coast.

Meteors

The 'shooting stars' seen on clear nights, especially at certain times of the year, are usually small particles from space which are vaporized by frictional heating as they enter the earth's atmosphere. It has been estimated that about a thousand million such particles plunge into our atmosphere every day. Occasionally, such bodies are large enough to reach the ground, when they are known as meteorites, but in most instances the diameter of a meteor is not more than about a millimetre. In 1923 F. A. Lindemann (later Lord Cherwell) and G. M. B. Dobson evolved a comprehensive theory of the vaporization of meteors, from which air density could be calculated at the heights of the appearance and disappearance of the flash. This work provided the first evidence for the existence of high temperatures in the stratosphere.

Meteor trails can also be located by radio and radar methods and it has proved possible to use these observations to estimate temperature, pressure, and wind at heights between 80 and 100 kilometres (50 and 60 miles).

Rockets and Satellites

As stated before, instrument-carrying balloons cannot be used above a certain level, but the rocket, being independent of the atmosphere, can attain any height. The region between about 25 and 50 kilometres is becoming of special interest to meteorologists, especially in view of the discovery that at great heights sudden large changes of temperature, known as 'stratospheric warmings', occur from time to time. There is need for a relatively cheap instrument-carrying rocket to extend radio-sonde measurements to greater heights.

In Britain, such a rocket has been developed by the Meteorological Office. It is about 8 feet long and carries in its detachable head a radio-sonde adapted for the measurement of temperature only and attached to a relatively large metallized parachute designed to open, on ejection, even in the very thin air at 50 kilometres. As the sonde and parachute fall, rapidly at first but more slowly nearer the ground, they drift with the wind and are followed by a ground radar station. In this way, winds can be measured to the top of the rocket trajectory. At the same time temperature is measured by a specially designed electrical thermometer whose indications are transmitted to earth by radio. As the radar data also give a continuous record of height, the final result is a fairly complete record of the state of the atmosphere up to 50 kilometres or even higher. A similar meteorological sounding-rocket is in routine use in the United States.

The artificial satellite offers unique opportunities for examining the atmosphere on the global scale by viewing it from without. Such satellites are really projectiles that are fired from the parent rocket at heights, speeds, and directions that ensure that they will remain in orbit, without further propulsion, for many months at least. In such an orbit, the earth is encircled in about 90 minutes at an average height of a few hundred miles.

So far, the main effort in this field has been the U.S. Weather Bureau's highly successful TIROS series. These transmit television pictures of sunlit areas of the earth's surface and of the clouds floating above them. Very large numbers of pictures have been received (over 10,000 in the first two years) and some interesting features have been seen. For example, a well-developed storm in the North Atlantic was found to have a spiral-band cloud pattern similar to a tropical hurricane, and although mountain wave-clouds* have been known for some time, the revelation of a series of regularly spaced clouds extending from the Andes Mountains across the South American continent came as a surprise. A dramatic success was the spotting of Hurricane Anna in 1961, several days before it was located and identified as a true hurricane by the usual methods.

The TIROS type of satellite produces pictures of clouds illuminated by the sun; they are not always easy to interpret, especially over a snow-covered landscape, but they have yielded particularly valuable information about compact well-defined atmospheric systems such as tropical storms and hurricanes that occur, for the most part, in poorly observed areas of the world, such as the tropical and sub-tropical oceans. The weather systems of the temperate latitudes have, in general, less well-defined cloud systems, and the British forecaster cannot expect to get as much help from satellite pictures as his colleague in the lower latitudes. Meteorological satellites will give the greatest immediate help in the study of global air currents, but there is no doubt that the establishment of a world-wide system of satellite weather watches must in time lead to major advances in all branches of the science. Such a scheme is now being planned by the World Meteorological Organization.

The methods described above may be regarded as the principal tools for the exploration of the stratosphere. At the

* See p. 72.

fringes of the atmosphere, radio propagation studies indicate 'winds' (drifts of electron clouds), and spectroscopic observations of the faint light of the night sky ('airglow') also give information. But for the practical meteorologist of today, preoccupied with the problems of the atmosphere near its lower boundary, these results are not of immediate interest. They are contributions to the stockpile of scientific knowledge which he hopes will be of use to those who follow in his footsteps.

PLANETARY ATMOSPHERES

As a postscript to this brief study of our atmosphere, it is of interest to see how the earth compares with other planets as regards its gaseous envelope. Despite many centuries of study, we still know little with certainty about the atmospheres of other members of the sun's family, but it is not difficult to see why some planets have substantial atmospheres and others have not, and also why certain gases which were probably present in the evolutionary stage of the earth's history are not now found in our atmosphere. As was stated in the opening sentence of this book, we retain a skin of gases by the force of attraction of the earth, but a closer examination of the matter shows that ability to hold on to an atmosphere indefinitely depends on a somewhat delicate balance involving gravity, temperature, and the nature of the gases concerned.

The molecules of a gas are in a state of incessant rapid motion of a random nature, the speed increasing with temperatures. To escape from the gravitational field of a body requires a certain minimum velocity (called the 'speed of escape'). Molecules having speeds of this order, or greater, if situated near the fringe of the atmosphere, are likely ultimately to depart into space despite the fact that their motions are random in direction, and this process, if continued long enough, must result in the eventual evaporation of the whole atmosphere into space.

If we know the nature and temperature of a gas we can easily calculate the *average* molecular speed, but this is not enough. Molecular speeds cover a wide range, and a statement that the average speed is so many miles a second implies that there are many molecules with speeds considerably in excess of this (and, of course, many with lower speeds). Jeans showed that if the average speed were not less than one-quarter of the speed of escape, the gas concerned would be almost entirely lost by the planet in the course of a few tens of thousands of years, an interval which is very brief on the evolutionary time-scale of the solar system. If, however, the average molecular speed did not exceed one-fifth of the speed of escape, the gas would be held fast by the planet for thousands of millions of years, which is a long time even on the astronomical scale.

With these criteria in mind, it is easy to see why the moon can have no substantial atmosphere, and a large cold planet like Jupiter, a very dense deep atmosphere. For our own atmosphere, the calculation makes it clear that hydrogen must have left us at a fairly early stage in the evolutionary process and why nitrogen and oxygen have been retained. The problem of helium, which is found in our atmosphere in significant amounts, is more complicated and cannot be discussed here, but broadly it may be said that the reasons for the permanence of the present constitution of the earth's atmosphere are known.*

We may thus conclude that the atmosphere of the earth must have existed in much the same form for a very long time and will remain substantially unchanged for an exceedingly long time to come provided, of course, that man does not commit the supreme folly of poisoning it with the products of his own ingenuity.

*See Smart, W. M. *The Origin of the Earth*. Pelican Books, 1955.

CHAPTER 2

The Atmospheric Engine

'WE regard weather as a series of incidents in the working of a vast natural engine.'* The implications of this statement become clearer when we consider the properties of water, the most important constituent of the 'working substance', as engineers call it, of the atmospheric engine.

Water, although an exceedingly common substance, is in many ways peculiar. In the first place, it is the only terrestrially abundant substance which exists simultaneously, and in the same locality, in all three phases, solid, liquid, and gaseous. Secondly, it is remarkable for its high specific and latent heats. (The specific heat of a substance is the amount of heat which has to be supplied or withdrawn to change its temperature by a fixed amount, and the latent heats measure the amount of heat set free or absorbed when a substance melts, evaporates, or solidifies.) Thirdly, water-vapour is capable of absorbing and emitting long-wave (infra-red) radiation easily, a property which is very important in meteorology. Finally (though this is not so unusual) water can exist for long periods in the atmosphere in the supercooled state, that is, as a liquid at temperatures well below 0°C. This property is of fundamental significance in the study of clouds and rain.

One result of these properties is that although the amount of water-vapour in the air is relatively small, never more than a few per cent of the total mass, its presence is highly significant because it acts as the main 'bank' of energy, by which heat is received, stored, and released, much as the banking houses of a country handle its income and

* Shaw, Sir Napier. *Manual of Meteorology*, III, p. 103. Cambridge, 1930.

expenditure. Water also provides the currency of the atmosphere in its energy budget, for it is mainly by water that the income from the sun is distributed over land and sea.

When the motion of the air over the earth is averaged over long periods, a quasi-permanent pattern, known as the *general circulation,* can be recognized. One of the major problems of meteorology is to trace the transformation of solar energy from the sunbeams to its ultimate appearance in the winds of the globe, and so to climate and weather. Although this problem has been studied for centuries, the solution is still far from complete, and in this chapter we shall attempt no more than an outline of the main features of the circulation and a sketch of some of the theories which have been evolved to account for them.

THE RADIATION BALANCE

Meteorology begins with the sun as the source of all atmospheric motion. For our purpose the sun is an unvarying source of heat, an incandescent globe 93 million miles away, with a surface temperature about 6,000°c. From the days of Newton it has been known that the light from the sun is made up of many colours, that is, contains radiation of many different wavelengths. It is customary to specify such wavelengths in microns (μ) or millionths of a metre, and for practical purposes, the radiation received directly at sea-level from the sun can be regarded as composed of waves whose length varies continuously from 0·3 to 2μ. The visible part of this spectrum lies between 0·36 and 0·76μ. Radiation of wavelength less than 0·36μ is called ultra-violet, and that of wavelength greater than 0·76μ, infra-red. Even at high-altitude stations such as Davos, in Switzerland, where the air is exceptionally clean, the ultra-violet radiation does not exceed about one per cent of the whole, and over 40 per cent of the energy in the solar spectrum is in the infra-red.

Only about half of the sun's output can be seen by us.

The solar beam constitutes the whole of the energy income of the atmosphere, the amounts received from the hot interior of the earth through the crust, and from the stars being negligible in comparison. At the fringe of the atmosphere the mean intensity of the solar beam is estimated to be 2 calories per square centimetre per minute, or about 135 kilowatts per square dekametre. It is unlikely that this rate, known as the *solar constant*, has changed appreciably in historical times. On the geological scale of time, the sun's radiation may have varied considerably, and at least one theory relates the ice-ages of the past to fluctuations in the solar constant.

By no means all of this tremendous output of energy is transformed into energy of motion. As stated in Chapter 1, the very short waves are stopped by the ozone in the stratosphere and over the globe as a whole about 40 per cent of solar radiation is reflected back to space, especially by clouds. Water-vapour absorbs about 12 per cent and the remaining constituents of the atmosphere another 5 per cent, so that, on the average, less than half of the energy reaching the fringe of the atmosphere gets through to the surface of the earth. Despite this, a beam of strong sunshine contains a great deal of energy, enough to raise the temperature of a column of air 3,000 feet high 3°c. in an hour, or to melt a slab of ice about a centimetre thick every hour, or to produce a normal lightning flash every day.

The incoming solar radiation must be very closely balanced by the outflow of radiant energy from the earth to space. Otherwise, the earth would be growing steadily hotter or colder, and climatological observations show no such long-term trends. The heat output of the earth, a much colder body than the sun, is entirely composed of infra-red or dark radiation, of wavelengths between 4 and 80μ. Such radiation is absorbed selectively by water-vapour – that is, water-vapour is transparent to radiation of certain wavelengths, opaque to others, and partly transparent to the remainder. This property of water-vapour makes the theoretical analysis of the heat balance extremely difficult, for the absorption spectrum of water-vapour in the far infra-red is very complex, so much so that it is only in the last twenty years or so that the spectroscopists have been able to present a complete picture. These studies reveal, among other features, the existence of a 'window' (a region of transparency) centred about 9μ. Such a window is of considerable importance in studies of the heat economy of the atmosphere because the energy of radiation from the earth reaches its maximum value at about 10μ, and much heat is lost to space in this band. It is sometimes difficult not to believe that nature conspires to deprive the earth of its heat, but water-vapour comes to the rescue by emitting radiation in the wavelengths which it absorbs. The return flow from the atmosphere to the earth plays an important part in the maintenance of surface temperature, and it is for this reason that ground frosts are more likely in dry clear air than in moist cloudy conditions.

Apart from water-vapour, the only constituent of the atmosphere able to absorb terrestrial radiation in significant amounts is carbon dioxide. The actual determination of the details of the heat balance depends mainly on the use of the long-wave absorption spectrum of water-vapour in conjunction with what is known of the distribution of water, as vapour or as cloud, throughout the atmosphere. On a global scale, data on the latter item are meagre. The atmosphere is thus crossed by a jumble of beams of incoming and outgoing radiation, with contributions from clouds and the air itself, a situation too variable and complex for exact analysis. Nevertheless, attempts have been made to solve the difficult problem of the heat balance, notably by the British meteorologist Sir George Simpson and by the American scientist

H. Elsasser. Both rely on very drastic smoothing of the irregular curve relating absorption by water-vapour to wavelength, Simpson by graphical methods and Elsasser by a mathematical function. One of the main results of these studies is to show that, on the average, from the poles to latitude 40° the outgoing radiation exceeds that coming in, and that from latitude 40° to the equator, solar radiation exceeds that lost to space.

There is thus over the continents and seas an uneven distribution of income and expenditure of energy. Because a balance exists for the whole globe, the atmosphere must incorporate within itself some means of compensation. The adjustment is made, in fact, by the general circulation and this is the genesis of the central problem of dynamical meteorology. Winds, clouds, rain, and other phenomena of weather are manifestations of the determination of the atmosphere to balance its budget.

THE ENGINE AT WORK

The atmosphere, as Shaw said, is a huge heat engine, a statement which becomes clearer when we consider how such engines work. Their essential features are that the working substance, usually a gas, is first compressed and then allowed to expand in an arrangement whereby the expansion is made to do useful work, such as driving wheels. In a steam locomotive, for example, the heat of the fire produces water-vapour at high temperature in the boiler, after which the compressed vapour is admitted to the cylinder where it is allowed to expand by pushing the piston forward. In expanding, the vapour cools, and the final expansion, to atmospheric pressure via the funnel, produces such intense cooling that the gas is instantly condensed to small water drops as a white puff. The two essential elements of a heat engine are a *source,* and a *sink,* of heat.

Part of the radiant energy received by the earth is transformed into the kinetic energy of the winds. In this way water is redistributed over the globe, a process essential for the continuance of life. Regarded in this light, the atmospheric engine is not very efficient in the strict technical sense. Not more than about 3 per cent of the energy received by the atmosphere (omitting the part reflected back to space as of no account) is transformed into energy of motion. For those who live in a moist cyclonic climate such as that of the British Isles such inefficiency matters little, but dwellers in arid or semi-arid climates, such as parts of Australia, North America, and Africa, are more aware of this aspect of nature's economy, and in recent years much effort has been devoted to 'rainmaking', the inducement or augmentation of precipitation by artificial means. We consider this matter in detail in Chapter 3.

The total energy of the general circulation has been estimated to be of the order of 10^{19} calories. This is very much greater than the energy released in the largest thermonuclear explosion to date, which explains some of the reluctance of meteorologists to attribute bad weather to nuclear weapon tests.

The starting point for all studies of the general circulation is the unequal heating of the earth's surface by the sun. The first problem is therefore to find out how temperature differences bring about horizontal motion. In a fluid, motion is initiated and maintained by differences of pressure, the flow, in the absence of other influences, being from regions of high to regions of low pressure. In hydrodynamics, the driving force is expressed in terms of the *pressure gradient*, defined as the difference in pressure between two points in the same horizontal plane divided by the distance between them. In the simple example of flow in a long straight pipe, the speed of the moving fluid is proportional to the pressure gradient along the pipe.

In the atmospheric engine, the tropics are the chief sources of heat and the polar regions, the sinks. Consider the simplest possible model, a flat, uniform non-rotating earth with such a 'source and sink' distribution of temperature (Fig. 4). Since we have no reason to suppose otherwise, we

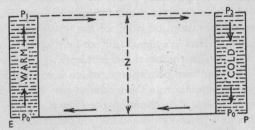

Fig 4 – Motion of the atmosphere caused by a
horizontal difference of temperature

must assume that pressure has the same value (p_o) at all points on the surface, so that initially no pressure gradient exists at the ground. Consider two columns of air, one, warm, over the equatorial region (E) and the other, cold, over the polar region (P). To find the pressure in the upper air at height z we must subtract from p_o the weight of the columns over E and P up to the height z. The column over E, being warm, is less dense and therefore weighs less than the column over P, and the pressures at height z must differ. In the notation of Fig. 4, p_1 (over E) is greater than p_2 (over P), so that air will move from over E to over P. Such a motion can take place only if there is ascent of air at E and descent at P, with a compensating low-level flow from P to E. A circulation is thus set up between the equator and the poles. We may look on this as the 'starting up' of the atmospheric engine.

Despite its highly idealized nature, this simple scheme has its counterpart in the real atmosphere. It is a general rule of meteorology that the pressure of the air high over a cold region tends to be below average and over a hot region, above average. A component of the motion of the upper air, called the *thermal wind*, can be attributed to the pressure gradient set up by the thermal gradient. A circulation of the type shown in Fig. 4 is believed to occur in the tropics and sub-tropics, with generally rising air near the equator and generally descending air about latitude 30°, but it is clear that the model cannot be valid for the whole globe. If such a simple situation prevailed, all surface winds would be from the north in the northern hemisphere, and from the south in the southern hemisphere, which is very far from the truth. We must elaborate the model to get closer to reality, and the first step is to abandon the 'flat stationary earth' concept and to consider instead motion on a rotating sphere.

Effects of the Earth's Rotation

The rotation of the earth has important consequences in meteorology apart from the alternation of day and night. In particular, the rotation explains why winds do not blow directly into the centre of a depression, but around it. A particle of air coming under the influence of a pressure gradient moves initially 'down the gradient' and would continue to do so indefinitely were it not for the spin of the earth. Except on the equator, the rotation causes the particle to swerve to the right of the direction of motion in the northern hemisphere, and to the left in the southern hemisphere. It is customary to represent this effect by postulating an apparent deviating force, called the *Coriolis force*, so that, except on the equator, a particle of air moving over the earth is subject to two forces, a driving force arising from the uneven horizontal distribution of pressure and a steering force arising from the rotation of the earth.

The Coriolis force is greatest at the poles and zero on the equator. It is proportional to the velocity of the particle, the angular velocity of the earth about its axis, and the sine of the latitude. Such a force acts on all bodies moving through the atmosphere. Ignoring air resistance, a projectile fired vertically with an initial velocity of 1,000 feet a second at latitude 60°N would fall back to the ground about 50 feet west of the firing point because of the spin of the earth. On the other hand, the Coriolis force is too small to be acceptable as an excuse for a bad drive in golf. In meteorology, the Coriolis deviation is a first order effect which, outside the equatorial regions, is decisive in regulating atmospheric motions.

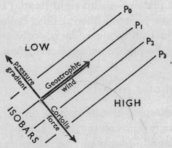

Fig. 5 – The geostrophic balance in the northern hemisphere

In time, the two forces acting on a particle, pressure gradient and deviating force, must come into balance. In these circumstances it is easily shown that, in the absence of friction, the resultant motion is along the *isobars*, or lines joining points with the same pressure, as in Fig. 5. Such a state of steady motion (that is, motion which does not change in pattern as time proceeds) is said to conform to the *geostrophic balance*, and the motion of the air along the isobars is called the *geostrophic wind*.

The problem of wind is considered in detail in Chapter 3, and for present purposes it is sufficient to say that the geostrophic balance is approximately satisfied on most occasions in the atmosphere. The theoretical geostrophic wind is a good approximation to the observed wind at heights of the order of 2,000 feet above a level surface, and any realistic analysis of winds over the globe must start with the fact that outside the equatorial zone the motion of the air is not along the gradient of pressure but perpendicular to it, that is, along the isobars.

For practical purposes, the effects of the earth's rotation are summed up in the famous law enunciated by the Dutch meteorologist Buys Ballot nearly a century ago. This says that an observer facing the wind in the northern hemisphere has the lower pressure on his right hand. (The law is reversed in the southern hemisphere.) Buys Ballot's law is one of the very few infallible rules of large-scale meteorology. It is never broken because the earth never changes its direction of rotation.

THE PROBLEM OF THE GENERAL CIRCULATION

If we could examine the motion of the air over the globe from the vantage point of, say, an artificial satellite, our first impression would undoubtedly be one of extreme complexity. In time, however, we should probably detect a drift from east to west in the equatorial and polar regions, with a general westerly current, much broken up by large eddies, elsewhere. The mean motion would be like that shown in Fig. 6. The arguments of the preceding pages can be used to account for the easterly motion in the equatorial belts, but far deeper considerations are needed to explain how the westerly motion arises and is maintained when it is flanked by winds in opposite direction and, like all motion of the air, is continually being reduced by friction.

When both the surface pressure and motion fields are considered, the broad features which call for explanation are as follows. Near the equator, pressure, on the average, is low and uniform and the weather is monotonous, with a prevalence of calms and light variable winds, occasionally

broken by squalls, heavy showers, and thunderstorms. This
is the region of the *doldrums,* notorious in the days of sailing
ships. At about latitude 30° lie the *sub-tropical high-pressure
belts.* Between these and the doldrums winds are generally
steady from the north-east in the northern hemisphere and
from the south-east in the southern hemisphere. These are

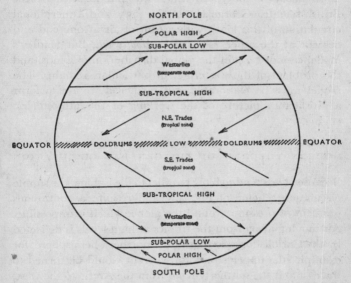

Fig. 6 – The distribution of wind and pressure over the globe (idealized)

the *trade winds,* the 'fair breeze' of the *Ancient Mariner.* * In
the sub-tropical anticyclonic belts winds are light and variable, but in the temperate latitudes the characteristic
feature is the broad belt of the *westerlies,* with abundant depressions and anticyclones, plenty of strong winds, and,
generally, very changeable weather. Nearer the poles are

---

* Coleridge's account of the meteorology of the trade wind and
doldrum regions accords reasonably well with fact, unlike his astronomy.

the *sub-polar lows,* associated with stormy weather, and ultimately, the *polar highs,* with a generally easterly motion.

The introduction of the earth's rotation into a thermal
circulation such as that of Fig. 4 explains how surface currents are deflected from a direct north and south motion to
winds from the north-east and the south-east respectively.
This theory of the trade winds was put forward by the
British scientist George Hadley in 1735, and a meridional
circulation of this kind, with ascent of air at one end and
descent at the other, is called a *Hadley cell.* But Hadley's
model cannot explain the global distribution of winds, and
the problem of the westerlies, in particular, remains. The
model must be elaborated still further if we are to form
a satisfactory picture of the working of the atmospheric
engine.

MODERN THEORIES OF THE GENERAL CIRCULATION

Because winds tend to blow parallel to the isobars, the simple
circulation scheme of Fig. 4 would require a continuous
gradient of pressure around the globe, which is impossible.
Air moving away from the tropics at high levels is deflected
by the Coriolis force so that in the northern hemisphere, for
example, the upper equatorial current would be turned to
the east and the southerly wind from the Arctic to the west,
thus causing a complicated circulation.

Angular Momentum

To probe further into the intricacies of the general circulation requires a closer examination of the consequences of
the fact that the atmosphere rotates with the earth but is also
free to move on its own. In technical language, the first
statement implies that the atmosphere possesses *angular momentum* about the earth's axis. 'Momentum' was introduced
by Newton to make precise the notion of 'quantity of

motion' and as such is measured by the product of velocity and mass. Angular momentum is the 'quantity of rotation' and is measured by the product of the angular velocity of a body and its moment of inertia. If the forces acting on a body have no leverage about the axis of rotation, the angular momentum of the body does not change with time. This is a cardinal principle, known as the law of conservation of angular momentum, which runs through physics from the atom to the cosmos. The mathematical formula shows that angular momentum is proportional to the rate of spin (angular velocity) and the square of the distance of the particle from the axis, and for any system of particles, whether rigidly connected as in a solid body, or free to move as in a fluid, but subject to internal forces only, then no matter how the configuration of the particles changes, the total angular momentum of the system about a fixed line in space is invariable. If, however, a particle of the system changes its position relative to the axis of rotation, its angular velocity must also change if the total angular momentum is to remain constant.

To illustrate this principle, suppose a man were standing on a horizontal turn-table which spins without friction about a vertical axle. His angular momentum is conserved, because the only external force is gravity, which has no leverage about the axle. The man could decrease or increase his rate of rotation simply by extending or dropping his arms, because in doing so he increases or decreases the distance of some parts of his body from the axis of rotation. A cat, falling feet uppermost, rights itself without pushing against a solid body by extending successively its fore and hind legs. This causes the body to rotate so that it lands on its feet, and the cat, in performing this feat, makes use of the principle of the conservation of angular momentum.

The angular momentum of a particle referred to the earth's rotation in space depends markedly upon its position relative to the axis, that is, upon the latitude in which it finds itself. In general, air has high angular momentum in the equatorial regions and low angular momentum in the polar regions, becoming exactly zero at the poles. It would thus appear that, ignoring friction, air moving horizontally from low to high latitudes must acquire increasingly high speed along the circles of latitude because of the conservation of angular momentum. (This is the counterpart of the man on the turn-table increasing his spin by dropping his arms.) Actually, nothing as simple as this can occur because of the combined effects of pressure gradients, friction, and the Coriolis force, but it is now generally accepted that there is a polewards transfer of angular momentum from the equatorial regions, reaching a maximum at about latitude 30°, in the sub-tropical anticyclonic belts. In the modern treatment of the problem of the general circulation the tropical and sub-tropical wind belts are regarded as sources of angular momentum, and much attention is paid to the mechanism of the transfer process.

The role of the polewards flow of angular momentum was first clarified by the British mathematician Sir Harold Jeffreys when he showed that the westerlies could be maintained by a flux of angular momentum from the lower latitudes. Without such a feeding-in of angular momentum, it appears that the westerly winds would die out in about ten days. The cyclones and anticyclones of the mid-latitudes are essential elements in the transfer process.

Jet Streams

In recent years, a new feature has emerged, partly to clarify and partly to complicate the picture of winds over the world. When observations at heights of the order of 40,000 feet are averaged, a sinous narrow belt of very high winds appears in the sub-tropics. The picture is that of a river of air encircling the globe, with speeds exceeding 50

knots (60 miles an hour) everywhere and in certain parts
reaching 100 knots or more. This belt of strong upper winds
is called the *sub-tropical jet stream*.

Nearer the poles, in the zone of the westerliés, the flow
pattern becomes very complicated. Some of the air in this
belt comes from the warm equatorial regions and some from
the cold polar regions. The surface of separation is known as
the *polar front.* When air currents with such very different
temperatures are in juxtaposition waves form on the front,
and may become the familiar depressions of the temperate
latitudes. This aspect of the air motion in the zone of the
westerlies is dealt with in greater detail in Chapter 4; here
it suffices to remark that in the mid-latitudes the general
circulation 'changes gear', with the depressions and anticyclones as the cogwheels. When winds át heights of the
order of 30,000 feet are averaged another belt of very high
speed appears. This has been called the *circumpolar jet stream.*

Meridional Circulation.

We are now in a position to assemble some of the pieces
of the jig-saw, although the result will be very far from a
complete picture. Fig. 7 shows the mean circulation from
the equator to the pole in winter in the northern hemisphere, based upon the analyses of the Finnish meteorologist
E. Palmén.

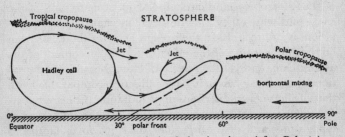

Fig. 7 – Mean meridional circulation in winter (after Palmén)

From the equator to about latitude 30°, conditions approximate to those in a huge Hadley cell, and this is the main source of angular momentum. At the northern end of the cell appears the sub-tropical jet. In the sub-tropical high-pressure belt there is generally descending air (subsidence). Part of this air is returned to the tropics by the north-easterly trade winds, and part goes north to join with the upper currents to form the westerlies. Some of the surface tropical air rises over the cold air to give the typical 'polar front' features. Finally, in the region between latitude 60° and the pole there must be considerable horizontal mixing of the air masses.

THE CONTINUING PROBLEM

Palmén's scheme is an admirable summary of existing knowledge, but like all theories of the general circulation it leaves many questions unanswered. By the use of three principles, those of the unequal heating of the earth's surface by the sun, the deviation of winds by the earth's rotation, and the conservation of angular momentum, it is possible to gain considerable insight into the way in which the global wind pattern develops and is maintained. However, there is still no completely satisfactory theory of the origin of the great zone of westerly winds under whose benign influence civilization has made its greatest advances, and the explanation of the sub-tropical and circumpolar jet streams, and of the exact part which they play in the maintenance of the circulation, is still to seek. In the present account there has been no specific mention of the effect of the water content of the atmosphere, and yet the release of latent heat by condensation is capable of exerting an influence comparable with that of the uneven distribution of radiation. Other important factors, as yet largely intractable, are the influences of topography and of the irregular distribution of land and water over the globe.

To some degree, the picture we have tried to present of a general circulation is a climatological fiction. It is a picture of a mathematical abstraction called the 'mean' flow, from which at any time the actual wind field may depart considerably. The sub-tropical high-pressure area, which plays such an important part in all theories, is not always clearly in evidence over the great land masses, although it is generally to be found over the oceans, especially in the southern hemisphere. There are also subsidiary wind systems, such as the Asian monsoons, which as yet cannot properly be included in a general scheme but which undoubtedly play an important part in the global system.

Two lines of attack on the problem are now exciting interest among meteorologists. One, involving the use of laboratory models, is a revival of an investigation initiated by the Austrian meteorologist F. M. Exner, who attempted to imitate the general circulation by water in a rotating bowl heated at the periphery (the equator) and cooled at the centre (the pole). The modern experiments are more elaborate, and the results more interesting, in that it has proved possible to reproduce in the model many of the features of the global wind pattern and, in particular, to produce thin sinuous belts of high-speed fluid resembling jet streams.

The second approach is by way of a mathematical model, using an electronic computer to carry out the laborious and complicated calculations. This work was initiated by the American meteorologist N. A. Phillips, who began with a set of hydrodynamical equations to represent motion in an idealized atmosphere. By their solution he hoped to throw light on the genesis of the real circulation, and the first results show considerable promise. Phillips found that if a small random disturbance were introduced into the simple primitive motion, the flow soon developed recognizable depressions and anticyclones in the mid-latitudes, with a sinous high-speed belt rather like the circumpolar jet stream. Such motions are still far removed from the complex patterns actually observed, but it is very considerable achievement to have gone as far as this by purely mathematical means.

The direct attack on the problem has not won through because of the complexities of the mathematics and also because air is essentially diluted water-vapour, the effects of which cannot be fully taken into account because as yet there is no technique adequate for the purpose.

We now take leave of the broader aspects and, in the next chapter, look at some of the details of the interactions between the water in the air and the sunbeams, which cause weather.

CHAPTER 3

Wind, Clouds, and Rain

WIND is the motion of the air over the surface of the earth. From the earliest times the poets have written eloquently of its fickle nature. 'The wind bloweth where it listeth' – hardly so, in the study of meteorology, but we may agree with the romantic writers in recognizing in the wind a characteristic element of random motion. In technical terms, the wind at ground level is usually highly *turbulent*, that is, consists of an endless succession of gusts and lulls with, simultaneously, rapid oscillations in direction. This property of the natural wind is more than a meteorological curiosity; it is a feature of the atmosphere on which life depends.

In the present chapter we shall be mainly concerned with the motion of the air averaged over periods long enough to smooth out the rapid fluctuations revealed by sensitive quick-response anemometers. The motion which results, called the *mean wind*, is strictly a fiction but is properly regarded as a 'representative value'. If a meteorologist commits himself to a statement that at a certain time and place the surface wind was 'south-west 10 knots', he means that the process of averaging the recorded motion of the air at about 10 metres above level unobstructed ground gave this velocity. During the period of averaging the record might show speeds varying between, say, 7 and 13 knots and directions between 210° and 240°, depending upon the locality, the weather, and the time of day. Such short period fluctuations are referred to as the 'gustiness' of the wind. Longer period averages can remove the details of the passage of depressions and anticyclones; the general circulation is an example of very severe smoothing of this kind.

Anyone who has looked at a weathercock with clouds
drifting high overhead must often have noticed a marked
difference in the directions of the two air streams, but the
full extent of the variation of the wind with height is evident
only in accurate meteorological records. From the early days
of the science, small free balloons filled with hydrogen
('pilot balloons') have been tracked by theodolites to determine the speed and direction of the air currents up to very
great heights. The method can be used only as long as the
balloon is visible and thus is useless when there is a great
deal of low cloud. Today, balloons are tracked by radar
in any weather and the art of following a tiny dot in
the sky through the telescope of a theodolite, so much
prized by the early meteorologists, has now largely fallen
into disuse.

One result of this work has been to show that a 'solid'
current, a wind that blows in the same direction at all
heights, is rare. The speed of the wind usually increases with
height, but even this rule is not invariable. Many of these
features can be explained by considering the combined
effects of the pressure and temperature distributions and the
deviating force arising from the rotation of the earth. The
geostrophic balance has been mentioned in the previous
chapter, and we shall now consider this principle in greater
detail as an essential preliminary to an understanding of the
way of the wind.

GEOSTROPHIC AND GRADIENT WINDS

When the pressure gradient and the effects of the earth's
rotation combine to give the geostrophic balance, the result is a very simple expression for the speed of the air, the
so-called geostrophic wind:

Speed of geostrophic wind = pressure gradient $\div$ $2\rho\omega \sin \phi$
where ρ is the air density, ω is the angular velocity of the

earth about its axis, and ϕ is the latitude of the place considered. The expression shows that the geostrophic balance
has no meaning on the equator, where, since $\phi = 0$, the
geostrophic wind would attain infinite values. In general,
meteorologists are reluctant to apply the principle of the
geostrophic balance within a belt extending about 10° of
latitude north and south of the equator.

On a weather map, the distribution of pressure is shown
by the pattern of the isobars, lines joining points with the
same pressure. The gradient of pressure is proportional to
the spacing of the isobars, and this allows the operational
meteorologist to evaluate the geostrophic wind very quickly
by means of a transparent scale graduated to allow for different spacing of the isobars. The method, which is self-
evident, is shown in Fig. 8, the effect of changes in latitude
being allowed for by corrections.

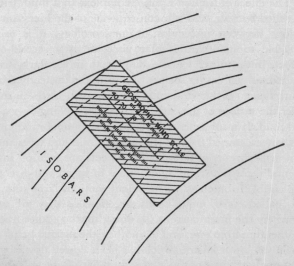

Fig. 8 – The evaluation of the geostrophic wind on the
forecaster's working chart

The geostrophic wind would be the true wind if we could ignore vertical motion, curvature of the isobars, and the effects of friction. As it stands, the expression is valid only for straight isobars, but air constrained to move on a circular path of radius r experiences an acceleration towards the centre of magnitude (speed)$^2 \div r$. With strongly curved isobars (for example, near the centre of a deep depression) this effect must be taken into account, and for steady motion the acceleration towards the centre must be provided for by the excess of the pressure gradient force over the deviating force. The result is that the speed of the wind required for the balance is reduced below the geostrophic value in motion around a centre of low pressure (depression) and increased above the geostrophic value in motion around a centre of high pressure (anticyclone). The corrected motion is called, not very happily, the *gradient wind*.

The effect of friction is more complex. In a fluid, friction is called *viscosity*, and is a consequence of the incessant collisions between molecules. In meteorology, it is usually possible to ignore molecular viscosity as a second-order effect, but another feature, similar to molecular viscosity but on a much larger scale, arises from the unsteady motion (turbulence) of the wind and cannot be neglected. Air moves over the surface of the earth like a car travelling over a rutted road. It is subjected to a rapid succession of random disturbances, caused by obstacles such as hills and trees and by upward currents of hot air. The effects are seen on instrumental records as rapid fluctuations in speed and direction, typical of turbulence. In turbulent motion, large lumps of air, called *eddies*, move in all directions as they are swept along by the main current. In doing so, the eddies transfer momentum from one level to another, the process being that air in the lower layers, which has been slowed down by the roughness of the ground, is mixed up with faster moving air from above, and vice versa. The ultimate result is a braking effect on the air as a whole. This feature of the natural wind, known as *eddy viscosity*, is far more effective than molecular agitation in producing frictional effects. To envisage the process, it is often helpful to think of the eddies in the wind as the macroscopic counterparts of the molecules in non-turbulent (laminar) flow, but the analogy is by no means exact.

When the term representing eddy friction is brought into the equation of motion, the balance is further upset and the resulting steady motion is no longer parallel to the isobars but slightly across, inclined towards the centre of low pressure. This theoretical deduction accords with observations, which show that in a depression the surface wind usually blows across the isobars at an angle of about 20°. At higher levels the effect of surface friction grows progressively smaller, and at heights between 500 and 1,000 metres (1,500 and 3,000 feet) over level country, is virtually nil. At these heights the motion is very nearly along the isobars, at a speed slightly below the gradient wind. This important result was demonstrated by the British meteorologist E. Gold in 1908 in a celebrated memoir entitled *Barometric Gradient and Wind Force*.

The geostrophic and gradient wind equations have some interesting theoretical consequences. In fluid dynamics the law of conservation of matter appears in the guise of the 'equation of continuity', which acts as a kind of watch dog on the calculations, by excluding all motions which would imply that matter is being created or destroyed by the flow. If it is also assumed that the flow is *incompressible*, that is, the motion does not change the density of the moving air, it follows that the pattern of flow must be such that nowhere does the air pile up or thin out. It is impossible to have horizontal flow into a region from all sides, and there must be an upward motion to prevent accumulation.

The geostrophic wind satisfies the continuity and incompressibility conditions without vertical motion – it is a strictly two-dimensional flow. The main phenomena of weather are essentially dependent upon large-scale up and down movements of the atmosphere, so that if the geostropic balance were exactly fulfilled, there would be no weather!

This conclusion is so remarkable, in view of the success of the geostrophic wind approximation, that some further explanation is called for. The reason is that, except in the vicinity of mountains or in thunderstorms, the vertical motion of the air is very slow. The normal rates of ascent and descent are rarely more than a few centimetres a second, compared with many metres a second for the horizontal motion. Vertical velocities in the free atmosphere (away from the surface) are usually two orders of magnitude below wind speeds and thus have little effect on the geostrophic balance. Nevertheless, because such movements are spread over immense areas, the mass of the atmosphere involved is very great and the effects on weather correspondingly significant. Much of the difficulty experienced in developing meteorology as an exact science arises from the fact that such vertical motions are 'unobservable' in the sense that no method can be devised to measure directly these small but exceedingly important movements with adequate accuracy over large areas.

The second property, which is a simple consequence of the gradient wind equation, is that although in theory wind velocities in a depression may attain any values, only a limited range of speed is possible in an anticyclone. In a region of high pressure winds must be light, and this is borne out by experience. Really high winds are necessarily associated with low pressure.

Thermal Winds

We have already seen that in the upper troposphere pressure tends to be low over cold regions and high over warm regions. The geostrophic wind at any height is now regarded as compounded of two motions, the geostrophic wind of the surface pressure field and, in the upper air, the 'thermal' wind, which is associated with changes in the pressure field caused by the variation of temperature with height. The thermal wind is thus the vector difference between the geostrophic winds at the two levels. The name, originally proposed by Gold in 1918, is derived from the fact that such motion is related quantitatively to the mean isotherms (lines of equal mean temperature) of the layer of air considered, in much the same way that the geostrophic wind is related to the isobars. The magnitude of the thermal wind is proportional to the horizontal gradient of temperature just as the geostrophic wind is proportional to the gradient of pressure, and it blows around the 'lows' and 'highs' of the temperature field in the senses indicated by Buys Ballot's law if we substitute 'temperature' for 'pressure'. In modern meteorology such mean isotherms are called 'thickness lines' (the reason for this nomenclature will appear later), and aerological charts, with cold and warm centres, now invariably find a place on the forecaster's bench.*

If the geostrophic wind does not vary with height the thermal wind is zero by definition. Such an atmosphere, called *barotropic*, represents a considerable idealization of the real atmosphere but is yet an important model for the mathematician.

In the mid-latitudes and the polar regions the thermal wind, more often than not, is westerly. As a consequence westerly winds at the surface tend to increase with height and easterlies to decrease. Southerly winds usually veer (change direction in a clockwise fashion), and northerly winds back, with height in the northern hemisphere. There are, of course, many exceptions to these rules.

* See Chapters 4 and 5. Hemispherical charts of thickness are published by the Meteorological Office in its *Daily Aerological Record*.

We shall now consider some of the more interesting special systems of winds.

TORNADOES AND HURRICANES

The highest wind speeds are found in *tornadoes*. The word comes from the Spanish 'tronado' (thunderstorm) and in north and central Africa still has this meaning. Meteorologists restrict the term 'tornado' to a special kind of disturbance, small in extent but characterized by fierce spiral motion around a well-marked vertical or nearly vertical axis. Such storms average a couple of hundred yards across, or even less. Photographs, such as Plate 1b, usually show a characteristic narrow black funnel extending from a low cloud base to, or nearly to, the ground.

Tornadoes occur all over the world, but most frequently in the United States and Australia. They are short-lived, with paths often not more than a few miles in length. Their destructive power is immense. There are no reliable records of the maximum speed reached by the whirling air because any anemometer which by chance was located in the path of the tornado is almost certain to be destroyed, but calculations made from studies of damage suggest speeds up to 300 miles an hour, and it is quite possible that this figure is exceeded on occasions. Pressure drops rapidly in the path of the storm; in Minnesota in 1904 a fall of 200 millibars (nearly 6 inches) was recorded by an aneroid barometer. A sudden reduction of this magnitude in atmospheric pressure could easily cause a building to explode outwards, and this kind of damage is typical of tornadoes.

The tornado is the nearest approach to the 'vortex' of hydrodynamics observed in the atmosphere and resembles in many ways the little whirlpool seen above the drainage pipe of a bath. But the origin and the true nature of tornadoes are obscure, despite the great mass of literature on the subject. Almost the only matter on which meteorologists are agreed is that the primary cause of tornadoes must be *atmospheric instability,* a term which requires some explanation.

It is natural to think that the equilibrium state of the troposphere, subject as it is to continual stirring by the winds, must be one of uniform temperature, but a little reflection shows that this cannot be true. In a state of perfect equilibrium it should be possible for air at different levels to be exchanged without affecting the balance as a whole. But a volume of air which is forced, for some reason or other, to move vertically must expand or contract because of the change of pressure with height. If it expands it cools, and since the adjustment for pressure is very rapid, the process is *adiabatic,* without transfer of heat to or from the surrounding air. Calculation shows that as long as the amount of water-vapour in the air is below the saturation value, adiabatic cooling takes place at the fixed rate of 1°C. for every 100 metres that the air is lifted. (The same arguments apply to heating by compression of descending air.) This result provides the criteria whereby we judge if the equilibrium of the atmosphere is stable or not. If the actual rate of fall of temperature with height (called the *lapse-rate*) is greater than 1°C. in 100 metres (this particular rate, called the *dry adiabatic lapse-rate,* is one of the constants of meteorology) a volume of air displaced upwards will always be warmer and therefore less dense than the surrounding air, for the upward moving volume can cool only at the adiabatic rate. Such displaced air is therefore likely to continue to rise indefinitely, a condition which is called 'unstable'. On the other hand, if the actual lapse-rate is less than the dry adiabatic rate, or is reversed (temperature increasing with height, a condition known as an *inversion*), air displaced upwards will always be colder and therefore denser than its surroundings, and will tend to sink back to its original level. This is described as a condition of *stability,* in which it is difficult, if not impossible, for upward motion to be sustained. The equilibrium state of the atmosphere is therefore one in which temperature falls with height at the adiabatic lapse-rate.

Large lapse-rates in the atmosphere well above the ground are usually associated with violent manifestations of the presence of strong upward currents, such as thunderstorms. How the intense instability, marked by very large lapse-rates, which seems to be the necessary forerunner of tornado activity arises is still a matter of debate. Such a condition might occur as a result of cold air overrunning warm moist air, or it might be a consequence of the rapid lowering of the base of cloud following very heavy rain. The long conical whirl, pendant from the cloud base, which is characteristic of tornadoes, seems to originate in a horizontal vortex in the cloud and its dark foreboding appearance indicates condensation of water-vapour by the sudden cooling of air expanding under the decreased pressure in the vortex. But there are many questions, such as the maintenance of the 'partial vacuum' at the centre despite the strong inflow at the surface, to which present-day meteorology can find no wholly satisfactory answers, and in the absence of a reliable theory the forecasting of the occurrence of tornadoes, and the prediction of their paths, is out of the question.

Hurricanes

In the original scale of wind force devised for sailing ships by Admiral Beaufort in 1808, the word 'hurricane' was used for a wind 'such that no canvas could withstand'. Later, a hurricane was defined as a wind whose mean speed exceeded 65 knots. In modern meteorology the name is reserved for a cyclonic disturbance of relatively small area, characterized by intense low pressure around which winds blow at very high speed. The more descriptive but cumbersome phrase 'tropical revolving storm' is often used in British official publications. The hurricane ranks with the tornado as a major destructive force and is more to be feared because, unlike the tornado, it is relatively long-lived and capable of causing widespread ruin should it move inland.

The characteristic features of the tropical hurricane, which serve to distinguish it from the familiar cyclonic depression of the middle latitudes, are its small size (the diameter of a hurricane is usually less than 100 miles, or about one-tenth of the mid-latitude depression), abnormally low pressure, high winds (often exceeding 100 knots), exceptionally heavy rain and thunderstorms, and the existence in all this turmoil of a central calm area, the 'eye' of the storm. The central pressure is usually about 960 millibars (28 inches), but 914 millibars (27 inches) was recorded in 1932 in the Caribbean Sea. The disturbance is usually symmetrical, with circular isobars. The storms usually form between latitudes 8° and 20° and initially they travel polewards and westwards and then eastwards. Most of the hurricanes of the Caribbean and West Indies areas ultimately die out or become sober depressions in the North Atlantic, but occasionally they penetrate into North America with devastating effect.

The birth and growth of a tropical hurricane present the meteorologist with many puzzles which are now being slowly unravelled. There are many rival theories, but it is generally agreed that the immense kinetic energy of these storms originates in the release of latent heat by the condensation of water-vapour, and this is borne out by the observation that hurricanes invariably form over warm seas, usually the western parts of the tropical oceans during their summer and early autumn, when there is a deep layer of warm moist air near the surface. No hurricane has ever been reported from the tropical parts of the South Atlantic and other low latitude regions where the sea surface is comparatively cool.

The tropics are usually regarded as regions of monotonously quiet weather, with steady trade winds, and the question immediately arises how intense disturbances can form in such conditions. Further, not all the storms that begin in these regions end up as fully developed hurricanes. The theory which follows is that of the American meteorologist Johanne Malkus*; it is not necessarily final or, as yet, generally accepted. It illustrates admirably the type of closely reasoned physical argument which is expected in modern meteorology.

Although the weather of the tropics is, on the whole, tranquil, this is strictly true of the surface layers only. Above 10,000 feet the homogeneity of pressure begins to give place to recognizable cyclones and anticyclones. This is in marked contrast to the temperate zones where the lower layers are the most disturbed and the upper layers, relatively tranquil. The Malkus theory places the origin of a hurricane in the upper air, beginning with the observation that from time to time easterly pressure waves, often 1,000 miles across, sweep through the trade wind current. The first result is a distortion of the trade wind and a characteristic sequence of weather. Ahead of the wave the weather is relatively clear with winds north of east; behind it are thick clouds and rain with winds south of east. The most important effect of the wave, however, is that it causes a break in the 'trade wind inversion', the surface of separation of the dry upper air and the moist lower air, which usually lies between 6,000 and 10,000 feet above the sea. In the neighbourhood of such a break moist air can ascend rapidly to form great masses of cumulus cloud towering to 50,000 feet. Such clouds often become raining thunderheads.

A very deep easterly wave can develop a vortex (Fig. 9),

* See, e.g., *The Scientific American*, August 1957.

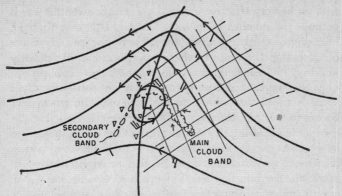

Fig. 9 – Distortion of the trade winds by an easterly wave,
with the formation of a vortex (after Malkus)

and this is the seed of the hurricane. Further growth of the
disturbance depends upon a number of fortuitous events. If
conditions are favourable, for instance if there is generally
high pressure in the surrounding air, there will be motion
into the vortex at the bottom and an outflow at the top.
This causes a reduction of pressure in the vortex and an
increase of the circulation with winds rising to moderate
gale force (35 to 45 miles an hour) accompanied by cloud
and thundery squalls. This is an incipient hurricane, and
most die before reaching maturity.

A true hurricane, unlike a mid-latitude depression, has a
warm centre. The formation of such a core of warm air is a
necessary but not sufficient condition for the growth to full
hurricane status because, in the first place, an inflow of less
dense air at the bottom is required to increase the wind
speed and, secondly, at the top, pressure must be higher
than in the surrounding air to provide a mechanism whereby the circulation can proceed unimpeded. The rise in the
temperature of the core is caused by the release of latent
heat by the condensation of water-vapour, but this process

will not be very effective unless the wet air is swept upwards without too much mixing with cold air. It is now that the breaking of the trade wind inversion by the easterly wave becomes significant, for by this means the clouds can quickly build up to great heights because of the intense convection.

At this stage, according to the theory, the formation of an 'eye' is the factor which decides whether the storm will become a true hurricane or not. The process described above is capable of raising the temperature of the air in the centre by perhaps two or three degrees c. At the centre of a true hurricane temperatures may be five or eight degrees c. above the surrounding air. The eye is a region some ten or twenty miles in diameter, free from cloud and wind but stiflingly hot and humid. In the eye, air descends and is heated by compression before being thrown out of the system by the centrifugal force of the whirling motion. Such a downward motion is the critical condition for the last stage in the production of a hurricane. Without it the temperature of the core cannot reach the high values necessary for the kinetic energy of the disturbance to rise above that of an ordinary storm. Once the eye forms and the associated heating of the air begins, the storm will develop the characteristic very low pressures and winds will attain true hurricane force. The theory thus envisages a series of crises in the growth of the hurricane, each of which has to be surmounted if the storm is not to end as a mere gale. This serves to explain why hurricanes are comparatively rare. The missing link in the theory is that no process is suggested for the formation of the eye.

Jet Streams

In 1923 a meteorological pilot balloon was seen to fall near Leipzig. It was found afterwards that it had been released four hours earlier in Hampshire, which meant that it had covered 570 miles at an average speed of 120 knots.

At the top of its trajectory the wind speed must have approached 170 knots (200 miles an hour). At the time such speeds were thought to be exceptional, but as the number and reliability of upper air soundings increased, it was realized that frequently there exist in the high levels of the atmosphere extremely fast rivers of air which meteorologists now call 'jet-streams'. The definition recently adopted by the World Meteorological Organization is: 'A jet-stream is a more or less horizontal flattened tubular current in the vicinity of the tropopause, with its axis on a line of maximum wind speed, and characterized by high wind speeds and strong traverse wind shears.* Generally speaking, a jet-stream is a few thousands of kilometres in length, a few hundreds of kilometres in width, and a few kilometres in depth; the wind speed is at least 30 metres a second (about 60 knots) at every point on its axis.'

This definition refers to what may be called 'local' jet-streams, not to be confused with the sub-tropical and circumpolar jet-streams described in the previous chapter, which are climatological features. Fig. 10 shows the vertical cross-section through a typical local jet-stream of the mid-latitudes. The thin lines are isokinetics, lines of equal wind speed, and the thick line is the tropopause, which is usually several thousands of feet higher on one side of the stream than on the other. There is an inner core of fast moving air (in this instance, exceeding 120 knots) between 30,000 and 35,000 feet, just below the tropopause. There is marked asymmetry; the wind shear is greatest on the left of the current and in the troposphere the colder air lies on the left, whereas in the stratosphere, above the wind maximum, the colder air lies to the right of the core.

To the left of the core and above it, where there are strong wind shears, the air is often very turbulent or 'bumpy'. In

* 'A strong wind shear' means that the speed increases rapidly over a short distance.

the high atmosphere, turbulence is usually found only near cumulonimbus clouds, especially those associated with thunderstorms. In the vicinity of jet-streams turbulence sometimes occurs without cloud, and is therefore difficult to

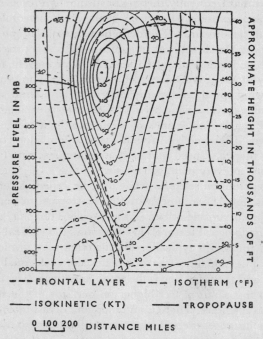

- - - FRONTAL LAYER   - - - ISOTHERM (°F)

——— ISOKINETIC (KT)   ——— TROPOPAUSE

0 100 200 DISTANCE MILES

Fig. 10 – Vertical cross-section of a local jet stream
(wind direction into page) (after Johnson)

avoid when flying, but fortunately 'clear-air turbulence' sufficiently severe to make a flight uncomfortable, or even dangerous, seems to be rare.

Local jet-streams are transient and seem to bear no simple relation to the weather at the surface. It is quite possible that a jet stream is roaring through the sky far above the reader as he turns these pages without his being aware of anything unusual in the weather. The presence of a jet-stream is an important fact for the forecaster as he ponders over the next stage in the development of a synoptic pattern, but he is unlike to associate any particular type of weather with its appearance.

Jet-streams are extreme examples of thermal winds, and the explanation of their cause which has won most support is the 'confluence' theory of the American meteorologists J. Namias and P. F. Clapp, put forward in 1949. The terms confluence and difluence are used to indicate flow towards and away from an axis, as with a narrowing or widening pipe. In synoptic meteorology, the terms refer to the geo-strophic wind, or flow along the isobars.*

Namias and Clapp suggest that jet-streams form in a region of confluence in which there is already a horizontal temperature gradient. An ideal situation of this kind is depicted in Fig. 11, in which temperature increases from the top to the bottom of the diagram. The effect of the con-fluence is to intensify the temperature gradient. The geostrophic balance then requires either that a belt of strong winds with a large vertical wind shear shall form in the upper troposphere, or that there shall be an op-posing belt of high wind near the surface. On most oc-casions the former situation prevails, since the atmosphere usually has already a general motion in the direction of the thermal winds. On this motion the new wind shear is im-posed, with the result that very high winds are formed but only in the upper troposphere. The motion is effectively limited at the tropopause because the temperature gradient in the stratosphere is generally opposed to that in the tropo-sphere. In this way it is possible to account for the characteristic features of the jet-stream, especially its tubular

* The words are not synonyms for 'convergence' and 'divergence', which are defined at length in Chapter 4.

form, high speed and location just below the tropopause.

Even in these days of powerful aircraft, jet-streams are important factors in the safe and economical operation of aircraft, civil and military. It is probable that jet-streams, then unrecognized as distinctive features of the upper air, played a part in the 1914–18 war. A fleet of Zeppelin airships, returning from a bombing raid on England, ascended

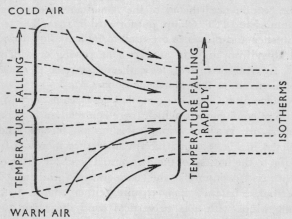

Fig. 11 – Formation of a strong temperature gradient by confluence (after Sawyer)

to 20,000 feet only to meet a northerly wind of 70 knots which blew them over France, where a number were destroyed. In our day, some of the more spectacular performances of aircraft can be attributed to the added push from a favourably placed jet-stream.

CONDENSATION PROCESSES IN THE ATMOSPHERE

In the older text-books of geography rain is usually explained by the statement that air which is forced to ascend, for example, by passing over hills, expands and thereby cools, with the result that its water-vapour is condensed into drops which fall as rain. Like many other popular statements about the weather, this explanation raises more questions than it answers. The problem which confronts the meteorologist may be put very simply thus: granted that the ascent of air causes condensation of the water-vapour into clouds, why is it that some clouds rain and others do not? Can we trace the history of a raindrop from its birth in a cloud to its ultimate fate as part of the water carried by the earth?

To answer these questions we must begin with some of the established facts about vapours in general. If a volatile liquid partly fills a closed vessel, the incessant activity of its molecules causes some of them to escape from the surface into the space above, which may or may not contain another gas. This is the process of evaporation. Eventually, an equilibrium state is attained in which the number of molecules of the liquid leaving the surface is equal to the number which return, and there is no longer a net loss of molecules from the liquid. The vapour in the closed space above the liquid is then said to be *saturated*; it exerts a definite pressure which increases rapidly with temperature, called the *saturation vapour pressure*. Evaporation ceases when this stage is reached.

It is important to note that the definition of saturation makes no reference to the presence of gases other than the vapour of the liquid in the space above the surface. In meteorology there has grown up a loose but inaccurate fashion of referring to 'saturated air', as if the atmosphere were a kind of sponge which can hold a certain amount of water-vapour and no more. It is not the air that is saturated but the water-vapour, and the pressure that the vapour exerts is independent of the presence of the other gases of the atmosphere. Nevertheless, the phraseology is convenient and sanctioned by long usage, and no harm is done in talking about saturated and unsaturated atmospheres as long as the speaker knows precisely what he means and is under no illusions about the alleged sponge-like character of air.

If the vessel is opened and the vapour allowed to diffuse into space, the number of molecules leaving the surface is unaffected but less return. The vapour is then *unsaturated*, and evaporation proceeds until no liquid is left. A vapour may also be made *supersaturated*, for example by the sudden cooling of saturated vapour. In this state, condensation is likely to occur, on the liquid surface or elsewhere. One of the first problems in the study of clouds is to ascertain the precise conditions in which condensation takes place.

At first sight this seems very simple and straightforward – apparently, all that is needed for the formation of a cloud or a mist is a slight degree of supersaturation. The real situation is far more complicated and interesting. In 1897 the British physicist C. T. R. Wilson showed that when moist air which has been freed as far as possible from foreign particles is subjected to a very large and rapid expansion, so that it is suddenly chilled and brought to the supersaturated state, condensation occurs only when supersaturation reaches several hundred per cent. Humidities of this order of magnitude are never encountered in the atmosphere (the maximum degree of supersaturation is a fraction of one per cent) so that the simple cooling of moist air cannot account for clouds, and still less for rain. We must look for some additional factor to promote condensation.

Condensation Nuclei

The process of condensation in the atmosphere turns on the presence of foreign particles which act, in a manner not yet fully understood, as centres for condensation. Such particles are called *condensation nuclei*. Their discovery was chiefly the work of the British physicist J. Aitken who, in 1880, showed that a cloud formed in a vessel containing slightly surersaturated air was made more dense when combustion products were introduced, but that when care was taken to remove all particles, the vapour could be made highly supersaturated without drops forming. Aitken concluded that when water-vapour condenses into drops in the atmosphere it always does so on the myriads of tiny particles (nuclei) present. He also realized that some particles are more efficient than others in promoting condensation.

Subsequent research has elaborated and confirmed many of Aitken's views, and it is now recognized that the normal abundance of condensation nuclei in the atmosphere prevents large supersaturations being attained at any time. The nuclei of the atmosphere consist of insoluble particles, soluble particles and 'mixed' nuclei, which are partly soluble, partly insoluble. As would be expected, soluble and mixed nuclei are more efficient than insoluble nuclei in promoting condensation. The size and number of nuclei in the atmosphere vary enormously. In ascending order of size, meteorologists now recognize 'Aitken' nuclei, 'large' nuclei, and 'giant' nuclei, with diameters ranging from a ten-millionth to a thousandth of a centimetre. Over the oceans there may be as few as a hundred nuclei in a cubic centimetre and, in the smoky air of an industrial area, several million in the same volume. The very small particles, because they require a high degree of supersaturation for condensation, probably play an unimportant part in cloud formation; the largest particles are significant in the production of raindrops.

Condensation nuclei are formed in three main ways: by combustion, by mechanical disruption (such as the formation of dust and sea spray), and by the coagulation of smaller particles into larger ones. Aitken suggested that fine particles of common salt, resulting from the evaporation of sea spray, would be exceptionally active in promoting condensation. There is no doubt that many of the nuclei responsible for cloud formation are produced in this way, but the belief is now growing that salt particles are not the main constituent of the really active nuclei. The British meteorologist B. J. Mason has estimated that only about one-tenth of the nuclei involved in cloud formation are salt. The remainder are chiefly mixed nuclei and the products of natural or man-made fires. *

Although smoke from domestic and industrial chimneys contains vast numbers of nuclei, atmospheric pollution is not the primary cause of fogs. Even if all the open fires in this country were extinguished, and motor vehicles ceased to run, we should still suffer from winter fogs. There are always plenty of nuclei in the air apart from the by-products of civilization. What pollution does is to make fogs denser and more persistent and, in the form of 'smog', more dangerous to health and damaging to property.

Supercooling

Before proceeding to the examination of cloud formation and the mechanism of rainfall, one other property of water needs to be considered. This is its ability to *supercool*, which it shares with many other liquids. The temperature of 0°C. or 32°F. is often called the 'freezing point of water'. It is more accurate to refer to it as the 'melting point of ice', and the difference is more than a matter of phraseology. Except at very low temperatures, water does not freeze unless it contains minute foreign particles. Very small drops of pure water, such as those found in high clouds, can remain liquid at temperatures well below 0°C. It has been estimated that only one cloud drop in a million is likely to freeze at temperatures between 0°C. and —10°C., and perhaps a few in ten thousand at —30°C., but all drops become solid below —40°C. A further important feature is that if a supercooled drop touches a fragment of ice, the whole mass freezes

* Mason, B. J. *The Physics of Clouds*. Oxford, 1957.

immediately. On the other hand, ice particles do not melt until the air temperature exceeds 0°c.

Water is by no means abnormal in this respect. It may surprise some readers to learn that glycerine, as purchased from a chemist, is a liquid in the supercooled state. The melting point of glycerine is 17°c. (63°F.), which means that although glycerine has to be brought to a low temperature to make it solid, a much higher temperature is needed to melt it again.

The importance in meteorology of this property of water cannot be over-estimated. In the upper part of the troposphere the air temperature is well below 0°c. Some of the high clouds are composed of ice crystals, but many contain vast numbers of supercooled water drops. Much of the theory of the formation of rain hinges on this observation.

CLOUDS

Professional forecasting depends largely on the rapid reporting of relatively simple observations over a large network of stations. In the international reporting code, clouds are classified according to their shapes, using the Latin names devised by the British chemist Luke Howard in 1803. Howard recognized three main types, high streak clouds which he called *cirrus* (Lat., a hair), heaped clouds, *cumulus* (a pile), and sheet clouds, *stratus* (a layer). The international classification adopted by the World Meteorological Organization has introduced many other names derived, for the most part, from the three main types given above.

The professional meteorologist must be able to recognize and name all types, but such detail is unnecessary for the general reader, and no attempt will be made to enumerate all the forms of cloud here. Scientific meteorology, although retaining much of Howard's classification for convenience, tends today to refer to clouds more in terms of the physical process dominant in their formation than by their appearance. It is customary, in scientific papers, to write of 'wave' clouds formed by air passing over hills, or of 'convective' clouds, as in thunderstorms. The most complete collection of cloud forms is that contained in the newly issued International Cloud Atlas of the World Meteorological Organization, but smaller collections also exist.*

The Formation of Clouds

The *dewpoint* of moist air is the lowest temperature to which it can be cooled at the same pressure without risk of condensation. It may also be defined, with greater precision, as the temperature at which the partial pressure of the vapour over a water surface reaches the saturation value. The dewpoint is thus a measure of the humidity of the air. A cloud is essentially the result of the chilling of moist air to a temperature below its dewpoint, and such cooling is normally caused by the ascent of a large volume of air. When air is cooled at ground level the result may be a mist or a fog. In this instance, the fall in temperature may be brought about by loss of heat by radiation from the ground.

As the air ascends, cooling proceeds at the dry-adiabatic lapse-rate (p. 55) until the dewpoint is reached. Condensation then begins and latent heat is released, reducing the rate of cooling to about half the dry-adiabatic value. At temperatures below 0°c. the cloud may contain ice crystals, or supercooled drops, or both. The subsequent history of the cloud depends largely upon the important difference between the *frostpoint,* defined as the temperature at which the water-vapour is saturated over an ice surface, and the dewpoint, which corresponds to saturation over a liquid (supercooled) surface. The dewpoint is lower than the frostpoint, a

* *Cloud Study*, by F. H. Ludlam and R. S. Scorer, published in 1957 under the auspices of the Royal Meteorological Society, is recommended as much for the clarity of its text as for the beauty of its photographs.

fact which is highly significant when the formation of rain is considered. We shall return to this important matter later, and here it suffices to remark that vapour which is saturated for a liquid water drop is supersaturated for an ice crystal.

Air may be forced to rise in several ways. The layer clouds of depressions are formed by the prolonged slow ascent of a deep widespread layer of air. This process is associated with *convergence*, the flow of air into the base of a region of low pressure. When rain is falling steadily in a mid-latitude depression the cloud layers can be as much as 30,000 feet thick and may extend over many thousands of square miles.

Convection can arise as a result of the heating of the ground by sunshine or by cool air blowing into warm regions of the earth. In both instances, large individual volumes of warm, moist air penetrate into cooler air and mix with it. The clouds formed in this way belong to the cumulus family and are easily recognized by their typical 'cauliflower' appearance. Such clouds usually have their bases at about 5,000 feet (the condensation level) and may tower to 20,000 feet or even higher. Showers of rain, hail, or snow often fall from the larger clouds. Within the clouds the ascending currents may be very powerful, and vertical motions of the order of 40 to 60 miles an hour have been measured in thunderclouds in America. Cumulus clouds are usually short-lived because of the continuous succession of evaporation and condensation caused by the vigorous turbulence, but the full extent of this activity can be realized only from 'lapsed-time' cine films, in which the scene resembles a vigorously boiling liquid. The analogy is more than literary, because the heated air ascends, not as a whole, but in the form of huge 'bubbles'.

When air is forced to ascend over a range of hills, quasi-permanent waves are formed to the lee. This feature has been the subject of some pleasant mathematical investigations, following the lines laid down by Kelvin in his famous study of wave patterns in a stream flowing over a corrugated bed. The waves give rise to typical lenticular clouds, gener- ally called *orographic* or *wave clouds*, and many local clouds, such as the Helm cloud of Cumberland, the Levanter of Gibraltar, and the Table Cloth of the Table Mountain, are of this type. A rare type of wave cloud, called 'mother-of- pearl', is sometimes seen high in the stratosphere over the mountains of northerly countries. These clouds have brilli- ant irridescent colours which are believed to be caused by the rays of the sun falling on supercooled drops.

Clouds are a fascinating and rewarding study for the photographer, particularly if he takes the trouble to learn something about the underlying physical processes. The detailed study of the physics of clouds has progressed greatly in the last twenty years, chiefly because it is now possible to study them in detail by radar and the use of specially equip- ped aircraft. The Meteorological Research Flight of the British Meteorological Office has led the way in this work, but space does not permit an account of the ingenious in- strumentation which has been developed by the M.R.F. to cope with the difficulties of taking samples of wisps of vapour several miles above the surface of the earth.

RAIN AND SNOW

The amount of water suspended in the air in the form of cloud is enormous. A small cumulus cloud, 'like a man's hand', may hold anything from a hundred to a thou- sand tons of water in suspension. A large cumulus cloud is a mountain of water drops and ice crystals, weighing perhaps a hundred thousand tons, and no meaningful figure can be given for the weight of the deep layer-cloud systems that accompany the depressions of the temperate latitudes.

It is not difficult to explain how such tremendous masses of water can remain aloft indefinitely. The minute drops that make up clouds, with diameters ranging from a ten-thousandth to a hundredth of a centimetre, apparently float in the air, but this cannot be true because water is eight hundred times denser than air. The drops actually fall, but at such a slow rate that their descent is virtually impercep- tible. All small bodies behave in this way in air, the reason being that the resistance of the air set up by the motion is sufficiently great to balance the weight of the drop or particle at very low speeds. In technical language, the 'ter- minal velocities' of cloud drops, which rarely exceed a few centimetres a second, are negligible compared with other motions affecting the cloud. If water is to fall from a cloud it can be only in the form of drops with terminal velocities hundreds of times greater than those of cloud drops.

The first problem in explaining rain is therefore to ac- count for the formation of large drops from small drops in- side the cloud. The smallest drops that reach the ground have diameters slightly greater than a tenth of a millimetre; this form of precipitation comes from low clouds and is called *drizzle*. Raindrops are one or more millimetres in dia- meter and are produced as steady precipitation by layer clouds many thousands of feet thick, or as showers from con- vective (cumulus) clouds. *Hail* is also produced by convec- tive clouds, and in hot climates may be centimetres in diameter. (There are authentic reports of hailstones as large as an orange.) *Snow* almost always falls from layer clouds.

An average raindrop represents the aggregation of about a million cloud drops. Any mechanism suggested for the production of rain must not only explain how this happens but also why the process is selective, for not all clouds rain. These are formidable problems, and the main difficulty for the meteorologist is no longer to explain how the water re- mains in the sky, but how it ever gets down!

One obvious solution is to assume that water continues to condense on the cloud drops until they grow large enough to fall out as rain, but this cannot be maintained. It is easily shown that this process acting on its own cannot produce drops much greater than a few hundredths of a millimetre in diameter, which would evaporate before reaching the ground. The simple condensation theory of rain must be abandoned.

The Bergeron Process

In 1935 the Swedish meteorologist T. Bergeron published a famous paper which not only described a plausible mechanism for the initiation and maintenance of rain but, indirectly, was responsible for the rise of 'rainmaking' as a commercial activity soon after the end of the Second World War. Bergeron began by examining all the processes which he thought might account for the presence of a substantial number of large drops in the middle of a cloud of very small drops All the different processes, such as electrical attractions between drops, were eliminated in turn as inefficient or too slow, and he was finally led to the conclusion that rain must begin as snow. He supposed that at the top of the cloud, where the temperature is below —10°C., there are vast numbers of supercooled cloud drops and relatively few ice crystals. (Even though water supercools easily, a few ice crystals are certain to form at temperatures below 0°C.) Ice crystals surrounded by supercooled water drops will grow at the expense of the drops for, as we have pointed out, vapour which is saturated with respect to water is supersaturated with respect to ice. In this way, water is distilled from the small drops to the ice crystals, and it has been estimated that a snowflake large enough to fall at an appreciable rate can form from about a million cloud drops in about 10 minutes. In falling, the snowflake reaches warmer air and melts into a raindrop. The growth of ice crystals at the expense of supercooled water drops is easily demonstrated in the laboratory, so that there is no doubt that the Bergeron process is physically possible. Further, the enlarged ice particles or snow-flakes throw off fresh particles of ice by splintering, so that the process is self-multiplying, and thus capable of explaining the ultimate production of large numbers of large drops from relatively few ice crystals.

The Bergeron theory has been welcomed by meteorologists and at one time it seemed plausible to suppose that all

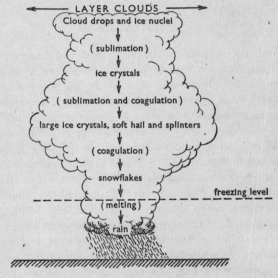

Fig. 12 – The Bergeron process

rain begins as snow, so that rain clouds must have their tops well above the level of the 0°c. isotherm. Radar studies have shown that most of the rain clouds of the temperate latitudes have snowflakes in their upper layers. But in the tropical regions showers often fall from clouds too warm to contain supercooled drops, and for this kind of rain a different mechanism must be postulated. It is now thought that in these circumstances rain is formed by the coalescence of smaller drops. A droplet bigger than its neighbours begins to fall, sweeping up smaller drops as it does so. In violent convection this process can be very effective in producing large drops and intense rain. There are thus two reasonable pictures of the formation of rain, one typical of the steady rain of the temperate latitudes, the other of the heavy showers of the tropics.

<h3 style="text-align:center">RAINMAKING</h3>

The Bergeron process can take place only if two conditions are satisfied: there must be in the cloud an abundance of supercooled drops and there must be some ice crystals among them to start the chain reaction. The earliest post-war experiments in rainmaking began with the 'seeding' of supercooled clouds by scattering pellets of an exceedingly cold substance, solid carbon dioxide ('dry-ice'), from aircraft on their tops. This followed the demonstration in 1946 by the American scientist V. J. Schaefer that a small particle of solid carbon dioxide produces hundreds of millions of tiny ice crystals when it is dropped into a vessel filled with a supercooled mist. Schaefer's experiment was soon followed by field trials in America and Australia, in which suitable clouds were seeded by several pounds of dry-ice pellets dropped by aircraft. There is ample evidence that such seeding produces, on most occasions, visible effects, and it appears that considerable volumes of supercooled layer and cumulus clouds can be converted into ice clouds by this method. In some instances there was evidence that precipitation, either of rain or snow, reached the ground.

The stimulation of precipitation for crops and water supplies by dry-ice dropped from aircraft has certain obvious limitations. It is expensive and restricted to small areas. In 1946 the American physicist B. Vonnegut made the important discovery that minute particles of silver iodide act as ice-forming nuclei at temperatures below —5°c. Vonnegut was led to try silver iodide because its crystalline structure is very similar to that of ice. Since that time it has been found that other substances, especially clay minerals and volcanic dust, act as ice-forming nuclei at temperatures above —40°c. (when water freezes without stimulation), but none are as effective as silver iodide.

The significance of Vonnegut's discovery for rainmaking lay in the fact that it is very easy to produce unlimited numbers of silver iodide particles by sublimation, for example, by injecting an acetone solution of the chemical into a hot flame or, even more simply, by burning coke impregnated with silver iodide in a brazier. If conditions are suitable, the silver iodide smoke should diffuse upwards from the ground into the supercooled parts of the cloud and the Bergeron process should be initiated.

At first sight it appears that this method of inducing re-calcitrant clouds to rain is ideal. Silver iodide is not particularly expensive and, in theory, only relatively small quantities are needed. The operation of seeding clouds from the ground is extremely simple. A line of generators, of the blowlamp or brazier type, is laid out many miles upwind of the target area and the emission of silver iodide is kept up for several hours, a task requiring only unskilled labour. The economic handicaps of seeding from aircraft are thus avoided.

Unfortunately, the simplicity of the method led to its commercial exploitation long before its effectiveness in stimulating precipitation had been investigated by disinterested meteorologists. There are many difficulties to be faced. In the first place, it is not certain that the silver iodide particles always reach the supercooled layers of the cloud, which usually are many thousands of feet above the ground. Smoke diffuses upwards fairly rapidly in the first few hundred feet of the atmosphere as a result of the turbulence of the surface wind, but at greater heights the process is much slower and may be stopped completely by an unfavourable temperature distribution. Secondly, silver iodide is affected by sunlight and loses its ability to nucleate at relatively high temperatures after about an hour or so of exposure.

In dealing with attempts to induce or augment rainfall, the major difficulty is that of assessing the results of trials. Rainfall is the most variable of all the quantities measured in meteorology. It is quite usual to experience successive wet and dry years, or to record heavy rain in one area and little or none a few miles away. The question which always arises after an apparently successful seeding experiment is whether nature, in fact, produced the rain without any stimulation by man.

There are two ways of testing rainmaking. One is to select an area for which accurate rainfall records have been maintained for long periods, at least thirty years. If, during a period of seeding, the observed rainfall exceeds the climatic mean given by the long-period records, statistical tests must then be applied to ascertain if the difference is *significant,* that is, not simply a chance result of normal weather fluctuations from year to year. The second method is to select two well-separated areas for which long-period rainfall records show a high correlation. One area is seeded and the other treated as a control. Comparison of precipitation in the two areas should then reveal if there is a significant difference in favour of seeding.

The practical difficulty is that both methods require a long sequence of trials for reliable results. This is a necessary consequence of the variability of rainfall and cannot be avoided. Even in the most favourable circumstances it is doubtful if worth-while results could be obtained from operations lasting less than three or four years. Many of the 'successful' seeding operations lasted only a few months and are thus useless as a means of judging the efficacy of the process.

In the first rush of enthusiasm, increases of several hundred per cent were claimed by some of the commercial operators. Today, such claims are generally discredited and it is thought that marginal effects, not exceeding 10 or 20 per cent increase, are the most that have ever been achieved, and even these modest results are open to grave doubt. To detect such small changes in a highly variable entity demands the most exacting statistical analysis of a long series of carefully controlled experiments. The verdict of the majority of meteorogists is that, despite the large sums of money expended on rainmaking, there is still no satisfactory proof that substantial increases in rainfall can be consistently produced over large areas by silver iodide released from the ground.

There is, however, a ray of hope. There is some evidence that a small but measurable increase in precipitation does occur when silver iodide generators are placed on the windward slopes of high mountains. The orographic clouds formed in such conditions are usually supercooled, and the uprush of air caused by the mountains should bring the silver iodide particles into the clouds rapidly and in good concentration. These circumstances give seeding by ground generators its best chance of success, but even for mountains as high as the Sierras of California, the results are not yet firmly established. In Great Britain, the mountains are hardly high enough for a similar result to be expected. Finally, it need hardly be said that there is no chance of breaking a long severe drought. Conditions must be suitable for natural rain before seeding can have any chance of success.

Research into nucleation is proceeding actively, especially in the Imperial College of the University of London. Some unexpected and fascinating results have already emerged, for example, that dust particles around which ice has formed once become even more efficient (that is, nucleate at higher temperatures) in initiating freezing in subsequent trials. It has been suggested that this effect is brought about by minute fragments of ice, trapped in cracks, which have survived the first melting and are thus able to act as promoters of freezing in the second trial. As yet, a true physical theory of atmospheric nucleation does not exist, either for condensation or freezing, and its ultimate formulation will no doubt require all the resources, not only of meteorology, but of crystallography and of physical chemistry. The question 'What causes rain?' is still one of the most difficult in meteorology.

CHAPTER 4

Depressions, Anticyclones, and Fronts: Prelude to Forecasting

THE mid-latitudes are characterized by prevailing westerly winds, changeable temperate weather, and precipitation all the year round. The day-to-day pattern of the weather is determined by the west to east movement of large-scale disturbances of the pressure field known as *depressions* and *anticyclones* (or *lows* and *highs*), with their associated *fronts*. In this chapter we shall consider the salient features of such dynamical systems.

EARLY MODELS

Modern meteorology is the child of the electric telegraph, and it is significant that the essential features of the structure of the extra-tropical cyclone were correctly described by Admiral FitzRoy, the first Director of the Meteorological Office, soon after simultaneous meteorological observations were brought into an international reporting scheme. As early as 1863 FitzRoy suggested that depressions marked the meeting of two great air streams with markedly different properties. One current, warm and humid, comes from the subtropics, and the other, cold and drier, from the polar regions, and he deduced that the typical depression forms on the boundary between the subtropical and the polar air. In view of the paucity of observations at that time, this must be reckoned as a most remarkable example of physical insight and there is little doubt that if these ideas had been followed up, meteorology, and forecasting in particular, would have advanced more rapidly in the nineteenth century than they did. But FitzRoy died in 1865 and his work

was temporarily forgotten. Meteorologists then were much
more concerned in exploring the anatomy of depressions, as
a preliminary step towards a practicable system of forecasting, and their preoccupation with this task may be ascribed
to the incessant public demand for forecasts at a time when
the science was not sufficiently developed for predictions of
weather to be made with confidence.

In 1887 the Hon. Ralph Abercromby, a gifted amateur,
published a classic of meteorology with the title *Weather*. In

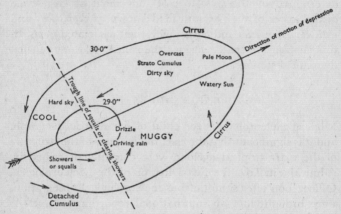

Fig. 13 – Abercromby's model of a depression (1887)

this book he gave a diagram (the essential features of which
are reproduced in Fig. 13) which identified the types of
weather found in the different parts of a typical mid-latitude
depression. For many years meteorologists elaborated this
kind of descriptive analysis in very great detail, but little or
no progress was made in elucidating the basic physical processes at work.

In 1911 the British meteorologists Napier Shaw and
R. G. K. Lempfert revived FitzRoy's ideas and made them
more precise. Fig. 14 shows their concept of the structure of

a depression. The feature which stands out most clearly is the discontinuity between different currents of air, and this may be one reason why the model did not find much favour at the time.

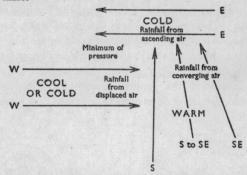

Fig. 14 – Shaw and Lempfert's model of winds
in a depression (1911)

THE BERGEN THEORY OF DEPRESSIONS

The crucial step towards a synthesis of these ideas into a coherent dynamical scheme was taken in Norway in the closing years of the First World War. A group of brilliant and enthusiastic meteorologists, working at Bergen under the inspiration of V. and J. Bjerknes (father and son) evolved the *polar front* or *Bergen theory* of the life-history of cyclones. The fundamental concept of the theory was that the typical depression of the temperate latitudes begins as a wave on the common boundary of two currents of different density flowing side by side. In Fig. 15(a) we have two such air streams, one easterly, cold and dense, from the polar regions, the other westerly, warm and light, from the subtropics. The surface of separation, called the polar front, is not truly horizontal but forms a wedge under the warm air, with a slope of about 1 in 100. On such a surface waves tend to form

and because of the strong shear across the front they may
grow in amplitude. The situation then becomes like that
depicted in Fig. 15(b). The warm current develops a bulge
with the cold air curling around in the rear. It is then possible to distinguish two parts of the front, the leading edge of
the tongue of warm air, called the *warm front,* and the
boundary of the cold air, called the *cold front.* The fronts
soon take the characteristic shapes shown in Fig. 15(c). This
is a *warm-sector depression,* and the reader should have little
difficulty in tracing the general resemblance between this
diagram and the far cruder picture suggested by Shaw and
Lempfert in 1911.

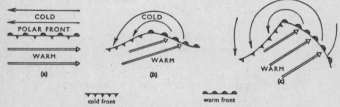

Fig. 15 – The Bergen theory of the birth of a depression

Fig. 16, which is based on one of the most celebrated
diagrams in meteorology, first published by J. Bjerknes and
H. Solberg in 1921, shows the depression in greater detail,
with the associated weather. The cold air ahead of the warm
front is in the shape of a wedge, and the less dense warm air
climbs the slope, cooling and condensing its water-vapour
into clouds, rain, and snow as it does so. In the rear, behind
the cold front, the dense cold air pushes beneath the warm
air, forming another cloud belt, usually not as wide as that
associated with the warm front.

The growth of the disturbance to this stage takes from
twelve to twenty-four hours. The second stage may take one
or two days more. During this period the cold front over-

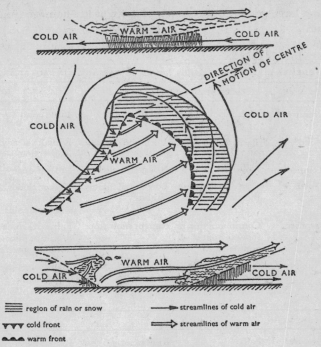

region of rain or snow   ➡ streamlines of cold air

▼▼▼ cold front   ⇨ streamlines of warm air

●▲● warm front

Fig. 16 – The warm-sector depression

takes the warm front, the warm sector disappears, and the depression is said to be *occluded*. Finally, all distinction between the air masses is lost and the depression ends its days

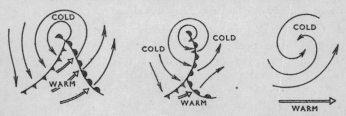

Fig. 17 – The final stages in the life history of a depression

as a large gently rotating mass of more or less homogeneous air.

ELEMENT	IN ADVANCE	AT THE PASSAGE	IN THE REAR
WARM FRONT			
Pressure	Falls steadily	Fall stops	Little or no change
Wind	Backs and increases	Veers and decreases	Remains steady in direction
Temperature	Slow rise	Rise continues	Little change
Cloud	Cirrus well ahead, then lower cloud	Low cloud, mainly nimbus	Higher clouds, stratus or strato-cumulus
Weather	Continuous rain or snow as front is approached	Rain or snow stops	Fair, with some drizzle or inter-mittent showers
Visibility	Good before the rain	Poor	Poor (sometimes mist or fog)
COLD FRONT			
Pressure	Falls	Rises rapidly	Rises slowly
Wind	Backs and in-creases, becoming squally	Sudden veer, often with heavy squall	Backs a little, then steady and veers in later squalls
Temperature	Fairly steady	Sudden fall	Little change
Cloud	Patchy, then con-tinuous; heavy towering cloud near front	Low dense cloud	Cloud lifts rapidly
Weather	Rain and perhaps thunder	Heavy rain, perhaps thunder and hail	Heavy rain for short period, fine with occas-ional showers
Visibility	Poor	Poor	Good

Fronts

The increased dissemination to the public of weather forecasts, especially by television, radio, and the press, has made the word 'front' commonplace. The table opposite* summarizes the behaviour of the elements of the weather in the vicinity of the fronts of a Bergen depression. There are no such clearly marked sequences of weather with the passage of an occlusion.

The sequence of weather described above has many points of resemblance with Abercromby's scheme (Fig. 13). Well ahead of the centre lie the cirrus clouds, familiar harbingers of bad weather. The detached cumuli and 'hard sky' of Abercromby are typical of the cold sector, and the squalls which characterize the cold front are also well marked. The sailor's rhyme,

> *When rise begins, after low,*
> *Squalls expect and clear blow,*

is an accurate description of the passage of a cold front. The 'clear blow' is the squally north-east wind accompanied by the lifting cloud and good visibility typical of the cold sector.

So far we have confined attention to the weather at the surface. Fig. 18 shows the isobars and the mean isotherms or thickness-lines of a warm-sector depression. These lines may be looked upon as approximations to the streamlines of the geostrophic wind near the ground and of the thermal wind aloft. The actual upper wind is the resultant of the surface geostrophic and the thermal winds. Ahead (to the east) of a developing depression the upper wind tends to turn into the north-west, and a well-known and usually reliable sign of the approach of a depression from the Atlantic is a strong movement of cirrus clouds ('mares' tails') in this direction.

* Adapted from *Meteorology for Aviators* by R. C. Sutcliffe (H.M.S.O.).

Hens' scratchings and mares' tails
Make tall ships carry small sails.

In the cold sector, the westerly thermal wind may oppose the surface easterly, giving a decrease of wind speed with height and often a reversal in direction. In the warm sector, the thermal winds blow in much the same direction as the surface winds, resulting in an increase of wind speed with height. At the cold front itself, the thermal wind component usually causes the wind to back with height.

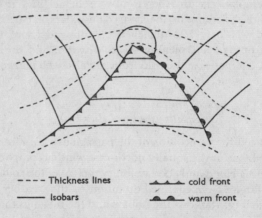

    - - - - Thickness lines   cold front
    ——— Isobars   warm front

Fig. 18 – Thickness lines and surface isobars

Flying through Depressions

Today, long flights are advertised as being 'above the weather', and it is true that flying through a depression no longer presents a hazard as it undoubtedly did in the early days of air travel. As a result of the elaborate international organization built up since 1920, the captain of an airliner is informed in advance of the position of disturbances and often he can plan his flight to avoid strong head winds or

bumpy air. A passenger who has some knowledge of meteorology can lessen the boredom of air travel by identifying
the different parts of a depression by the cloud sequence. The
first sign of a depression is cirrus cloud several hundred
miles ahead of the warm front. If the flight continues towards the front, the clouds will thicken and ultimately may
extend to within a few hundred feet of the ground. The
passage through the warm front is marked by the cessation
of rain and a general clearing of the upper cloud, but the
passenger may not be aware of all this unless the aircraft
descends to make an intermediate stop. Flying at a considerable height in the warm sector is usually smooth, but may
lack interest because the ground is often obscured by cloud.
The approach to the cold front is marked by high or medium
cloud, gradually thickening to a dense dark band on the
horizon, but at heights above 15,000 feet there are usually
only detached heads of cumulonimbus, which the pilot
avoids because of bumps. The most disturbed conditions are
limited to a belt about twenty miles wide, after which the
weather becomes clear, but although flying conditions
generally improve, the air remains bumpy and squalls are
likely to occur for some distance in the cold air behind a
depression.

Air Masses

The concept, originally evolved by FitzRoy and extended
by later workers, of the depression being the meeting ground
of air streams with characteristic properties, is now familiar
in meteorology. In general, weather is controlled by temperature and humidity, and it is the rule rather than the
exception to find on a weather map large areas over which
these elements show relatively little change. A part of the
atmosphere having substantially the same physical properties over a large area is called an *air mass*, and it is customary
to refer to a mass by its origin. Modern meteorological

literature abounds in references to polar and equatorial (or tropical) air, and there are many subdivisions, such as maritime polar, continental tropical, and so on, in order to take account of the changes which an air mass undergoes during its travel. In general, air of tropical origin is warm and moist, especially if it has come a long way over the sea. Such air is liable to low cloud, fog, and drizzle. Tropical air which has passed over a large land mass is drier and usually fairly free from cloud. Polar air generally is cold and relatively dry, with much broken cloud, and is often marked by squally weather with showers and perhaps thunder, but much depends on the surface over which it has travelled. 'Maritime polar air' is usually fairly humid and liable to cloud; 'continental polar air', on the other hand, is dry and not as liable to showers.

Although the air-mass concept is essential for the understanding of modern meteorology, it would be wrong to leave the reader with the impression that a volume of air which has been labelled 'polar' or 'tropical' must always have certain closely defined properties. The descriptions given above are generalizations; they are about as valid as an account of the inhabitants of Wales as short dark people with melodious voices and a passion for rugby football. In the process of analysis which must precede forecasting, it is essential to distinguish between the main air streams which in many ways seem to be struggling for mastery. The word 'front', brought into meteorology during the First World War, reflects this concept. The basic dynamical idea of the Bergen meteorologists was that the kinetic energy of the extra-tropical cyclone is derived from the difference in potential energy of polar and tropical air masses in contact. The depression and its winds are the means whereby the atmosphere reduces this inequality of potential energy, and the polar front theory of cyclonic disturbances is an attempt to explain the mechanisms of the process.

ANTICYCLONES

An anticyclone is a region of high pressure characterized by light winds or calms and generally quiet weather. Rain is unusual, but drizzle sometimes occurs. In the British Isles fine settled weather in summer is usually associated with a north-eastwards extension of the semi-permanent Azores anticyclone. Days are warm and brilliantly sunny, and skies are clear except for some detached convective (cumulus) clouds in the afternoon. Such summers, re-collected in age as the halcyon days of youth, give rise to the familiar myth that the weather is not what it used to be.

Anticyclonic weather is not always as pleasant as this. In winter an anticyclone often results in the sky being covered with a thick uniform sheet of cloud which, with the weak sunlight, produces the condition known to meteorologists as 'anticyclonic gloom'. The cloud sheet is associated with a marked temperature inversion, brought about by the upper air sinking and warming by compression. Such subsidence is very slow, but may go on for days, with the result that the inversion persists only a few thousand feet or less above the ground. When this occurs the surface air is effectively shut down by a 'lid', for an inversion checks rising currents. Into this imprisoned air domestic and industrial chimneys, motor vehicles, and railway engines pour smoke. The cessation of upward motion, coupled with the light winds or calms typical of anticyclones means that the natural ventilation of cities and industrial areas is reduced to a very low level, or ceases, and polluted persistent fogs ('smogs') may form. The great London smog of 1952 is still the outstanding example of this evil, but it had one good effect in that it gave rise to the Clean Air Act.

In addition to the two main types of pressure systems the weather forecast often refers to certain minor systems such as a 'ridge' of high pressure or a 'trough' of low pressure. A ridge frequently travels in much the same direction as the wind across it, but this is not a rigid rule. The weather of a ridge is usually fine, especially when the ridge is situated in the polar air behind a depression.

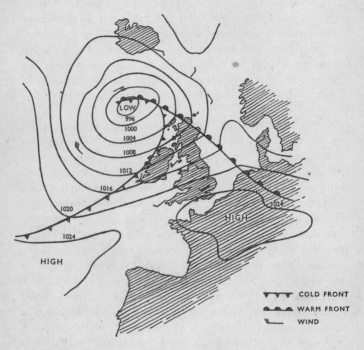

Fig. 19 – Warm-sector depression over the British Isles (19 May 1958)

Sharply V-shaped troughs are usually associated with fronts, but troughs can also appear when no front can be found. In such instances it frequently happens that a secondary depression forms in the trough.

So far, the illustrations have been of idealized weather

systems. Figs. 19 and 20 show actual charts, but it must be admitted that to find a 'text-book' depression of the type shown in Fig. 19 necessitated a search through a large number of charts. In most instances the situation is far more complicated.

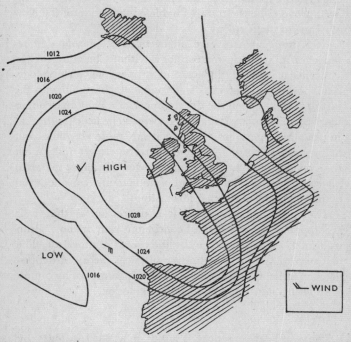

Fig. 20 – Winter anticyclone over the British Isles (19 February 1958)

DYNAMICS OF WEATHER

The account of the birth, life, and death of a depression given in the preceding pages is necessarily an idealization, and although some extra-tropical disturbances follow the .

theoretical pattern closely, many do not. The main achievement of the Bergen school was to gather together and make
precise ideas that were implicit, but not fully realized, in the
work of pioneers such as FitzRoy, Margules, Shaw, and
Lempfert. The model also suggested new and fruitful open-
ings for the mathematicians and, in the long run, this may
well prove to be the most valuable contribution of the Nor-
wegians to meteorology.

It is impossible to give an account of present day re-
searches in synoptic meteorology without bringing in the
concepts of fluid dynamics and its peculiar terminology.
The most significant work in dynamical meteorology in the
last decade has been the development of a truly mathematical system of forecasting. There seems to be little doubt that
in time this type of prediction will supersede all others, but
at present forecasting depends more on expert judgement
than on calculation. An account, however brief, of the main
physical theories is an essential prelude to any consideration
of the technique of weather forecasting.

The outstanding fact about a depression is that it is
accompanied by widespread continuous rain or snow. Rain
is formed, as we have seen, by the ascent of moist air. The
first step towards a quantitative physical theory of depressions must be an examination of the dynamics of a column
of air with a slow but definite vertical motion.

Divergence

The word 'divergence' is used in a narrow sense by
meteorologists and with a wider connotation by mathematicians. Fig. 21 gives some examples of the horizontal lines
of flow in what meteorologists call 'divergence' and 'convergence'. In divergent flow, fluid moves out from a centre,
and in convergence the reverse occurs – fluid moves into a
central region. It is clear that if these diagrams are representative of conditions at the base of a column of air, in

neither case can the motion be entirely horizontal. Air cannot accumulate or thin out indefinitely in any portion of the atmosphere, and if convergence takes place on a substantial scale near the surface, there must be widespread upward movement of the air as well. Similarly, low-level divergence over a large area is associated with generally descending air, a process usually called *subsidence* in meteorology. Fig. 22

Fig. 21 – Examples of (*a*) convergence and (*b*) divergence

shows vertical sections of convergent and divergent motion fields, typical of cyclones and of anticyclones. In general terms, air flows into the lower levels of the atmosphere in a region of rainy weather, and out of the lower levels in an area of dry weather.

A difficulty of phraseology enters when these matters are dealt with by the established methods of fluid mechanics.

In mathematics the 'divergence' of a motion is a scalar (non-directional) function which measures the rate at which fluid flows into or out of an area or a volume. The mathematical term thus covers equally what the meteorologist calls 'divergence' and 'convergence', the difference being one of sign only. In practice, the double meaning rarely causes confusion, but in the account which follows we shall, when necessary, distinguish between 'divergence' in the meteorological sense and 'divergence' as a mathematical function.

The barometer measures the weight of air above a region of the earth's surface, so that the rate of change of surface

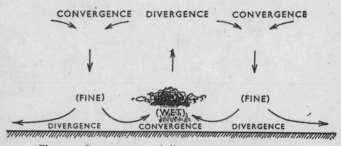

Fig. 22 – Convergence and divergence in the atmosphere

pressure must be related to gains or losses of air by the column as a whole. The relation between the time rate of change of pressure at the surface and the integrated horizontal divergence of the winds in the air above is called the *tendency equation*. By its use we can deduce some significant facts.

Except in very intense disturbances, such as tornadoes or tropical hurricanes, the rate of change of surface pressure is always small, not more than a few millibars an hour, and often much less. When such values are inserted in the tendency equation, it follows that the total divergence (in the mathematical sense) in a column of air is always very

small. This result, however, tells us nothing about the way in which air flows in and out of the column at different heights, and it might well happen that the smallness of the net divergence is the result of a near balance between a large convergence at low levels and a large divergence at high levels. This is what happens in most of the depressions of the middle latitudes, the divergence (in the meteorological sense) above a developing depression being slightly greater than the convergence at the surface, so that the total change of mass in the column arises from a small residual divergence. This explains the paradox that surface air flowing into a region is associated with a falling, not a rising, barometer.

The patterns of Fig. 22 show that regions of divergence and convergence must be adjacent (otherwise continuity could not be maintained). The divergence function must change sign at least once in a column extending from the surface to the limit of the atmosphere. Hence there must be an intermediate *level of non-divergence*, for a continuous function cannot change sign without passing through zero. This level plays an important part in the dynamics of cyclones.

A further simple mathematical argument shows that the divergence in a column of air can be expressed in terms of the rate of change of vertical motion with height. If the winds were strictly geostrophic there could be no vertical motion or, in other words, a geostrophic wind system is non-divergent.* No matter how the isobars widen or contract, the magnitude of the geostrophic wind keeps in step with the spacing, just as water filling a pipe flows more rapidly where the pipe narrows and slows down where it widens, so

* This is equivalent to the statement that the geostrophic velocity satisfies the equation of continuity in two dimensions, and is strictly true only if the variation of the Coriolis parameter with latitude is ignored. This approximation is justified for systems of relatively small dimensions such as the extra-tropical depressions.

$$\nabla \cdot u = - \frac{\partial \omega}{\partial z}$$

that there is no piling up of fluid at any point. Departures from the geostrophic balance, small though they may be, are of primary importance in the study of weather.

One factor which causes the wind to depart from the geostrophic value is the friction of the ground, which makes the wind blow slightly across the isobars, instead of along them, as with the true geostrophic wind. This effect must cause air to rise over a centre of low pressure and to descend over a region of high pressure, but calculation shows that friction by itself cannot produce sufficient convergence to account for the widespread continuous rain or snow of a vigorous depression. The problem must be investigated more deeply, and this necessarily brings in one of the fundamental concepts of hydrodynamics, which plays a role in fluid motion comparable with that of angular momentum in the dynamics of solid bodies.

VORTICITY

In the mathematical analysis of fluid motion, divergence plays a fundamental part. The divergence function is a scalar quantity formed from the spatial derivatives of the velocity components. Another equally fundamental function formed from the derivatives of velocity components is that which measures the amount of rotation in a fluid. This quantity is a vector called the *curl*, but in problems of hydrodynamics rotation is so important that it is known by the special name of *vorticity*.

The word 'vorticity' immediately suggests a 'vortex' or whirlpool, but the technical term is not restricted to such dramatic circumstances. Fluids tend rather easily to go into a spin, and nearly all natural motion, of air or of water, involves rotation. Irrotational motion is primarily a mathematical concept which is approached closely only in carefully controlled laboratory experiments. A difficulty which the non-mathematician finds in reading accounts of fluid dynamics is that vorticity can exist in motion which seems at first sight to be devoid of rotation (such as flow in a straight pipe) and yet not to exist in phenomena with apparently contradictory names such as 'irrotational flow around a cylinder'.

The difficulty vanishes when it is realized that in fluid mechanics, vorticity always measures the rotation of *infinitesimal* elements of the fluid. Such elements, or fluid 'particles', are mathematical concepts which bear no relation to the molecules which make up a real fluid. In order to make use of the techniques of the calculus, the mathematician supposes that a fluid can be subdivided without limit into tiny blobs which, however small, still possess bulk properties such as density or temperature. This means that for the purpose of calculation it is assumed that fluids such as air are continuous media.*

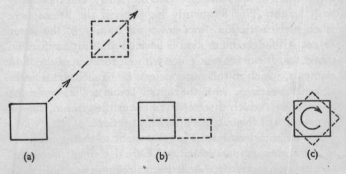

(a) (b) (c)

Fig. 23 – Translation, deformation, and rotation of a fluid element

Suppose that such an infinitesimal particle is represented by a square, as in Fig. 23. The square can be moved parallel to its sides. This is a motion of pure translation

* For a discussion of this matter see the author's *Mathematics in Action*, 2nd ed., London, 1957.

which involves no rotation. The square can also be deformed into an oblong or other shape without changing its area. This again involves no rotation. Finally, as in (c), the element may be rotated. In general, when a real fluid moves, its elements are translated, deformed, and rotated simultaneously, but it is possible for a fluid to move along a curved path without its elements being rotated. To see how this can happen, consider the 'giant wheel' of the fun-fair. The cars attached to the circumference of the wheel are suspended on hinges so that they remain upright during the motion. If we imagine the cars to represent fluid particles, this illustrates 'irrotational motion around a centre'. If the cars were rigidly attached to the wheel, their motion would cease to be irrotational.

The more perplexing circumstance of rotation in an apparently irrotational motion is illustrated by the example of a broad 'solid' current of air, in which the wind blows everywhere in the same direction but with speed increasing with height. This frequently happens in the atmosphere when surface friction slows down the motion in the lower layers. Although the motion is horizontal, a little reflection shows that it cannot take place without rotation of the fluid elements, which in this instance can be likened to an array of roller bearings, with the upper layers rolling over the lower layers, which themselves roll over the ground. This is an example of vorticity generated by friction.

For technical reasons it is convenient to define vorticity as twice the angular velocity of a fluid element about an axis through its centre. The axis may point in any direction; in the example of the wind near the ground given above the entire rotation is about a horizontal axis, but in general there will be three components of vorticity about the horizontal and vertical axes, respectively.

The large-scale weather systems of the troposphere have a marked two-dimensional character, and it is possible to regard rotation in such systems as taking place almost entirely in the horizontal plane. In other words, when dealing with the dynamics of depressions and anticyclones, rotation about the vertical axis, or the vertical component of vorticity, is far more important than the components about the horizontal axes. (This may be regarded as a consequence of the relative shallowness of the troposphere.) However, for motion on this scale, the most interesting and important result arises when the atmosphere is viewed from outside the solar system. Usually, motion of the air is measured relative to the earth's surface, but the atmosphere also rotates with the earth. An observer on, say, one of the fixed stars would therefore regard calm air as possessing vorticity, and would add this amount of vorticity (which varies with distance north and south of the equator) to the vorticity which the air might possess as a result of its movement relative to the ground. Meteorologists use the term *relative vorticity* for twice the angular velocity of a fluid element about a vertical axis fixed in the earth, and the term *absolute vorticity* to denote the sum of relative vorticity and the quantity $2\omega \sin\phi$ (ω = angular velocity of the earth, ϕ = latitude), which is the vertical component of vorticity arising from the diurnal rotation of the earth. Except near the equator, the two terms are comparable in magnitude, for in the large-scale weather systems the rate of rotation of a fluid particle does not usually exceed a few revolutions a day.

The Conservation of Absolute Vorticity

If the motion be regarded as horizontal and free from friction, it is possible to show very simply that the fractional rate of change of the absolute vorticity of an air particle as it moves over the surface of the earth is equal to the divergence of the motion. This connexion between vorticity and divergence, called the *vorticity equation*, is perhaps the

$$\frac{1}{\Omega}\frac{d\Omega}{dt} = \nabla \cdot \underline{u} = -\frac{\partial w}{\partial z}.$$

most important single relation in dynamical meteorology. It is fundamental in numerical forecasting.

The divergence of the winds is always small and becomes zero when the motion is assumed to be geostrophic. In these circumstances the vorticity equation reduces to the statement that the absolute vorticity of a volume of air remains unaltered as it moves. In meteorology this is known as the *principle of conservation of absolute vorticity*, and like all conservation relations in meteorology, must be regarded as an approximation to reality based upon an idealization of the atmosphere. However, the reader can see the reasonableness of this principle by considering what happens to an eddy which is formed, for example, on the surface of a slow running river by a jumping fish. Such an eddy is almost entirely two-dimensional, and as it drifts downstream it is evident that it tends to preserve its spin for a considerable distance. This is the counterpart of what happens in the atmosphere.

These considerations are strictly valid only for hypothetical atmospheres. Vorticity is generated in real fluids by internal friction, or viscosity. If the atmosphere were truly devoid of friction, vorticity could not be formed in any motion which was originally irrotational, and equally, any motion of a frictionless fluid which contained vorticity would continue to possess it unchanged for ever. Lord Kelvin, who discovered the theorem of the permanence of irrotational motion, was so impressed by these properties that he proposed a theory of atoms, then regarded as uncreatable and indestructable, as vortices in the luminiferous aether which was supposed to pervade all space.

In any fluid, vorticity tends to be concentrated into relatively small regions, and may be transferred from one place to another, either by bulk motion or by the diffusing action of turbulence. At a front in the atmosphere there is a large shear because of the different winds in the adjacent air masses. In such circumstances vorticity reaches a maximum intensity in a narrow band which approximates to the ideal state known in fluid dynamics as a 'vortex sheet'.

In the dynamics of depressions, the relation between vorticity and divergence is all important. When air which has relatively low vorticity moves towards the centre of a depression, it ascends and its vorticity increases. This is very much like the example given on p. 41 of the man on the turn-table increasing his rate of spin by pulling his arms into his sides, and this is the physical meaning of the vorticity equation. These facts are highly significant in practical meteorology, for although it is almost impossible to estimate divergence directly from wind observations, it is practicable to estimate, by graphical methods, the rate of change of absolute vorticity from consecutive weather maps.

Development Theory

The most important work of recent years on the relation between vorticity and divergence in weather systems is that of the British meteorologist R. C. Sutcliffe who, in 1947, discovered a mathematical relation which not only clarified the whole picture of cyclone dynamics, but did much to open up the way for 'numerical' forecasting.

Between 1914 and 1925, the British meteorologist W. H. Dines, who was one of the pioneers in the exploration of the upper atmosphere, recognized that divergence above a deepening depression exceeds convergence at the lower levels. The important factor is thus the difference between the divergence (in the mathematical sense) at two levels. Sutcliffe used this fact in conjunction with a simple cyclonic model with divergence in the upper troposphere and convergence lower down to analyse the process of cyclonic development in relation to vorticity.

Suppose that in Fig. 24, h_0, h_1, h_2, and h_3 are approximately horizontal surfaces in the atmosphere, with h_0 very near the ground and h_3 at a great height. If there is convergence on h_0 there must be divergence on h_2, say, with ascending air between. At very great heights (h_3), there will be convergence again.

The level h_2 will be in the upper troposphere, and at some intermediate level (h_1), divergence must vanish, with the ascending currents reaching a maximum value. This is the level of non-divergence (p. 97), estimated to coincide

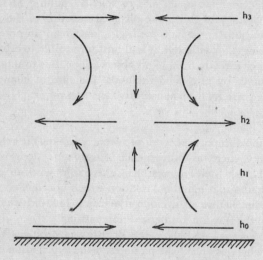

Fig. 24 – Sutcliffe's theory of development

with the 500-millibar surface which in the mid-latitudes is about 18,000 feet above sea-level, or roughly mid-way between the surface and the tropopause.

The mass-balance in the stratum between h_0 and h_2 will depend mainly on what happens on the bounding surfaces, for conditions on h_3 can have little effect because of the low air density at great heights. Sutcliffe measures *development* (D) by the difference between the divergence (in the mathematical sense) of the winds at the levels h_0 and h_2. If D is positive (more air being lost on h_2 than is gained on h_0), cyclonic development is said to occur. If D is negative, the development is anticyclonic.

If a relatively small effect arising from changes in latitude is neglected, the development function D can be separated into two terms which have simple physical interpretations on a weather chart which displays both surface isobars and thickness lines (mean isotherms). One term involves the thermal wind and the rate of change of the vorticity of the surface wind field measured in the direction of the thermal wind. The other term contains the product of the thermal wind and the rate of change of the vorticity of the thermal wind field measured in the same direction. These quantities are called the *thermal steering* and the *thermal development* terms, respectively.

To see the significance of this dissection in terms of forecasting, consider a warm-sector depression with thickness lines lying nearly straight and parallel over the warm sector (Fig. 19). The vorticity of the surface wind field is then dominant in the expression for D, which is positive (cyclonic development) ahead of the depression in the direction of the thermal winds and negative (anticyclonic development) behind. Hence the rule that in such cases the depression moves with the thermal wind, a process known among professional forecasters as 'thermal steering'. If the thermal wind near the centre and the surface wind in the warm sector are in much the same direction the rule coincides with a much older empirical rule that the centre of a depression often moves parallel to the surface wind in the warm sector. The thermal development term depends entirely upon the pattern of the thickness lines and often makes a notable contribution to cyclonic development.

The development theory throws considerable light on the way in which the atmosphere redistributes its vorticity. The complete motion of the atmosphere arises as a result of the superposition of two separate motions, one derived from the surface pressure distribution and the other from the thermal pattern, which varies with height. Changes in vorticity in any region may be classified as those arising from the advection (horizontal movement) of vorticity with the surface flow and those arising from the advection of the thermal pattern. The first kind are called *barotropic changes* and the second, *baroclinic changes*. These concepts have had considerable influence on the development of purely mathematical methods of forecasting.*

Long Waves in the Atmosphere

Pressure waves of many kinds travel through the atmosphere, but most of them have no perceptible influence on the weather. Sound waves are mere ripples of pressure, and, despite the popular belief that the noise of gunfire causes rain, their intensity is much too low to affect weather in any way. A very large explosion, such as that of the volcano Krakatoa in 1883 or, in our own day, that produced by a thermonuclear weapon, causes the atmosphere above the source to be lifted temporarily. The resulting disturbance, something like a hump on the surface of water, is propagated as a 'gravity wave' and, as with Krakatoa, may be detected far from the source as a jump on the records of sensitive barographs. Such waves travel at speeds not very different from that of sound (about 700 miles an hour) and here again there is no evidence that they affect weather in any way.

The waves that affect weather are of large amplitude and move slowly. In 1940, the Swedish meteorologist C.-G. Rossby showed that waves of this description can form in a slightly disturbed circumpolar air stream because of the variation of relative vorticity with latitude. In all the

* See Chapter 6 for a more detailed explanation.

preceding discussions the change of the Coriolis parameter with latitude has been ignored, a simplification which introduces no significant error in studies relating to relatively small areas of the earth's surface. It is otherwise for motions on the global scale.

We have already explained that the time-rate of change of absolute vorticity is related to the 'mathematical' divergence (p. 101). In a horizontal barotropic motion the rate of change of absolute vorticity is zero because there is no divergence. This is the law of conservation of absolute vorticity. But absolute vorticity is relative vorticity plus the term $2\omega \sin \phi$, which varies with latitude. If a particle of air in an otherwise steady circumpolar current starts a polewards motion as a result of a small disturbance, its relative vorticity must decrease if absolute vorticity is to remain unchanged. This means that the motion of the particle becomes progressively less cyclonic (or more anticyclonic) and ultimately it will be deflected back towards the equator. On this stage of its journey the reverse process takes place, until once again it moves towards the pole. The process is shown diagramatically in Fig. 25. The relative vorticity changes sign regularly, so that air particles in a slightly disturbed

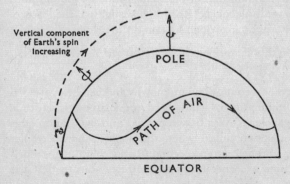

Fig. 25 – Long waves in the atmosphere

westerly current execute oscillations in latitude. Such a motion is called a *Rossby wave*.

The argument given above is intuitive, and the question immediately arises whether such theoretical phenomena have any counterpart in the real atmosphere. The atmosphere is not exactly baratropic and absolute vorticity is not truly conserved. If these difficulties are ignored, does what remains yield any clue to the processes which occur in the real atmosphere?

Rossby's simple but illuminating analysis begins with a steady uniform zonal wind blowing from west to east around the globe. In this current he introduces a small disturbance, and then calculates the form of the waves which arise because of the change of relative vorticity with latitude, as explained above. It turns out that the speed of propagation is related to the zonal wind speed by a very simple expression:

$$\text{speed of waves} = \text{speed of zonal current} - \beta \, (L/2\pi)^2$$

where β is a quantity, called the Rossby parameter, which measures the rate of change of the Coriolis parameter with latitude,* and L is the wavelength. Thus the waves travel at a speed less than that of the zonal wind. To gain an idea of the magnitude of L, Rossby investigated the case of stationary waves, for which he found the simple expression:

$$\text{wavelength of stationary waves} = 2\pi \sqrt{\frac{\text{wind speed}}{\beta}}$$

This expression contains no unknowns and can be evaluated for any combination of wind speed and latitude. In latitude 60° the wavelength lies between 3700 and 8300 kilometres (2,300 and 5,200 miles) when the zonal wind speed lies between 4 and 20 metres a second (8 and 40 miles an hour.) These results are encouraging, for they indicate that the

---

* Actually, $\beta = 2\,\omega \cos \phi/R$, where R is the mean radius of the earth.

variation of relative vorticity with latitude can affect phenomena on the scale of depressions and anticyclones in westerly currents moving at speeds corresponding to those actually observed. Rossby's result may also be expressed in the equivalent form that there is a critical zonal wind speed for which the wave becomes stationary. In latitude 60°, the critical speed for a disturbance of wavelength of 4000 kilometres (2,500 miles) is about 5 metres a second (10 miles an hour). The critical wind speed increases as the wavelength increases or the latitude decreases. Waves of relatively short length are propagated forwards, but as the wavelength increases, the wave first becomes stationary and then retrogressive.

From the magnitudes involved, it is clear that there could be at the most only five or six such waves around the hemisphere at any time. The evidence for the existence of Rossby waves is to be found in the upper air. Near the surface of the earth, and also at great heights, the well-defined dynamical systems are small, usually of dimensions between 1,000 and 3,000 kilometres (600 and 2,000 miles). In the mid-troposphere the motion of the air is appreciably simpler and the disturbances are on a larger scale. On the 500-millibar surface (about half-way between the surface and the tropopause in the mid-latitudes) it is usually possible to find oscillations of the Rossby type, and there are often four or five indentifiable long waves on a hemispherical chart. In applying Rossby's criteria for the progression of the waves the forecaster confines his attention, for the most part, to the motion pattern at about 20,000 feet.

The study of the magnitudes associated with a simple type of perturbed motion in a highly idealized atmosphere thus leads to results which can be related to the winds displayed on the upper-air charts of the forecaster. The idea that an approximation to the path followed by a volume of air can be calculated on the simple assumption that its absolute vorticity remains unchanged has proved remarkably fruitful in the development of purely mathematical methods of forecasting. These methods are described in Chapter 6, but before we consider this approach we must know something of the way in which forecasts are made in the traditional manner. This is the subject of the next chapter.

CHAPTER 5

Professional Forecasting

THE forecasting of weather is one of the many professional activities of meteorologists. Outside the profession it seems to be believed that the practice calls for a great deal of 'weather wisdom', an instinct for detecting coming changes normally attributed, in varying degree, to sailors, shepherds, and cows. The professional forecaster works with charts and spends little time in scanning the horizon; his personal reactions to the atmosphere around him matter very little. The official weather forecast is designed to be, as far as possible, an objective assessment of probabilities based on a survey of the physical properties of the atmosphere over large areas and to great heights.

THE NATURE OF FORECASTS

Apart from describing newly discovered phenomena, all physical sciences are preoccupied with prediction and verification. The sequence of observation, theory, idealization, mathematical development, and final verification by comparison of theory with controlled experiment has dominated Western science since the days of Galileo and Newton. Forecasts of weather have only a slight connexion with this scheme. In the laboratory the physicist is able to set the stage for his experiments and to bring in only those characters in whom he is interested. The meteorologist is more like a critic who, arriving well after the play has begun, has to recognize the characters, pick up the threads of the plot, and at intervals dash out to telephone to his paper an account of what has happened, and his opinion of what is likely to take place in the next act. The elimination of unwanted effects, which is the basis of all laboratory work, is impossible in geophysics and this accounts for most of the difficulties experienced in making advances in this region of physical science.

Prediction in the uncontrolled sciences varies enormously in precision and accuracy. A forecast of the date, time, and belt of totality of an eclipse is infallible, and predictions of tides are nearly as good. At the other extreme, there is no known method which allows an earthquake or a volcanic eruption to be foreseen, and the most that can be said is that these events are less likely to occur in some countries than in others. Forecasts of weather lie between these two extremes, not nearly as good as astronomical and tidal predictions but far removed from the purely negative deductions of seismology and vulcanology.

Weather forecasting is a profession which has to be run on business-like lines to meet the demands of aviation, the armed forces, industry, and the general public. For this a large reporting and analytical organization is needed, both nationally and internationally. Behind this immense effort is the science of meteorology, with its research groups, international services, university departments, and institutes.

Why are forecasts needed, except to satisfy curiosity? There are very few human activities, apart from summer sports, that are absolutely dependent on the weather. Mankind does not need detailed forecasts of all the changes in the weather during the next twenty-four hours to survive, or even to live comfortably. Forecasts are provided by governments mainly for economic reasons, and the field covered is very wide. The civil air lines need chiefly information about upper winds over many different routes, with details of visibility at the terminal points; the farmer is interested in surface conditions, chiefly rain, wind, and frost; and the housewife would like to be told about good 'drying days'. To meet these diverse demands the operational forecaster must try to predict, not instantaneous or even average values of all the meteorological elements, but 'representative values'. A weather service is to be judged, not by the volume of the data it supplies, but by their usefulness and reliability.

The heterogeneity of meteorological phenomena necessitates the use of observations made simultaneously over a wide network of stations linked by an efficient system of communications. In this respect, if no other, meteorology is unlike astronomy, which is adequately served by a few widely spaced observatories. The density of the meteorological network is limited by its cost and the amount of information which can be digested by the forecasting services. The number of stations and the frequency of the observations partly control the amount of detail which can be given in a forecast, but meteorology itself imposes a limit. The weather map, even when drawn every hour from observations made over a network as dense as that in Great Britain, cannot reveal the fine-structure or all the transient small-scale phenomena of weather, such as convective showers and thunderstorms, and it is for this reason that the official forecasts speak only of showers 'here and there' or of the 'likelihood' of thunder.

The only features that can be 'seen' on the charts of the operational forecasters are large slowly-moving weather systems with linear dimensions of the order of hundreds of miles. Professional forecasting is founded on two established facts: that such systems are sufficiently persistent to allow their movements and developments to be predicted for periods of about twenty-four hours, and that associated with these systems are characteristic physical phenomena, such as precipitation, that constitute weather. The association between a disturbance and weather is not unique – the passage of a front does not always result in the exact sequence of weather given on p. 86, and there must be, in any honest forecast, a certain amount of imprecision which reflects the properties of the physical system being considered and not the desire of the forecaster to cover all eventualities by 'hedging'.

A forecast of the type 'Tomorrow, at X, rain will commence to fall at 12.46 p.m. and cease at 3.32 p.m.' belongs to the realm of science fiction. Such precision is impossible, not because of lack of skill or industry on the part of meteorologists, but because the motions of the atmosphere, which is essentially a fluid in turbulent motion, are not predictable to such limits so far ahead, particularly in the mid-latitudes. Claims have sometimes been made for successful predictions of the details of the weather (for instance, the exact state of the sky) at a particular locality many days before an important event. In all such instances success or failure is a matter of luck, and an honest forecast for a period of twelve hours or more in the temperate zone can be only a broad statement of the most probable course of the weather with the knowledge that the reliability of the prediction must decrease sharply after the first twenty-four hours. No one who understands the true nature of atmospheric dynamics would claim more.

The present chapter deals exclusively with short-range forecasts, having a period of validity of not more than twenty-four hours with a possible 'further outlook' for forty-eight or seventy-two hours. Long-range forecasts, valid for periods of the order of weeks or months, involve different techniques and are dealt with separately, in Chapter 7.

All professional forecasts are based on synoptic charts, which show weather conditions over a large area at fixed times. 'Synoptic meteorology' is generally understood to comprise the study of the physical systems revealed by such charts, usually in sequence. 'Physical meteorology', on the other hand, is concerned with the details of the processes taking place in the atmosphere, such as evaporation and condensation. The synoptic meteorologist thus sees the drama of the weather in a series of instantaneous pictures, to which he must add the element of continuity with a guess at the nature of the next picture that is coming into view.

THE ORGANIZATION OF FORECASTING

There are five divisions of labour in the preparation of a forecast:

> Observations
> Communications
> Display and manipulation
> Analysis
> Prognosis

Observations

Nearly every country in the world maintains a network of stations for observing and reporting weather according to an international plan. In Europe alone such stations are numbered in thousands, mostly at airfields, health resorts, and observatories. Some of the more important centres provide observations every hour of the day and night; others report at three-hourly intervals with times synchronized in Greenwich Mean Time according to international arrangements.

Surface observations, which are by far the most numerous, consist of readings of properly exposed barometers, thermometers, and anemometers, with eye observations of weather (precipitation, visibility, cloud). Upper-air observations are now made regularly by radio-sonde and radar-wind apparatus* supplemented by data from aircraft on special meteorological reconnaissance or from civil aircraft on scheduled flights. There are eight upper-air stations in the United Kingdom, making observations of pressure,

* See Appendix.

temperature, and humidity twice daily, and of upper winds four times daily. Reports of weather over the oceans come from merchant ships on voyages and from Ocean Weather Ships. There are nine Ocean Weather Stations in the North Atlantic, at which ships specially equipped to make meteorological observations, including radio-sonde and radar-wind ascents, take position. Because of the great depth of the Atlantic the ships cannot anchor but steam slowly around the position for a period of two or three weeks before they are relieved. The work, which is organized internationally by agreement between countries which operate regular air passenger services across the Atlantic, is arduous and monotonous, but its values to forecasting can hardly be overestimated.

In addition, lightning flashes are located by a special network of 'sferic' stations, and in this way it is possible to fix the position of thunderstorms with fair accuracy up to 1,000 miles away.

Communications

The observations are transmitted over the meteorological communications network in the form of a five-figure code, of which the following is a sample:

99903 772 82930 48605 93251 36226 48518 83706 85725 87560

Decoded, this reads:

At London Airport the whole sky is covered by cloud. The wind is blowing from 290° at a speed of 30 knots. Visibility is 3 miles, there is intermittent slight rain and there has been drizzle in the past three hours. The pressure is 993·2 millibars and the air temperature is 51°F. The medium cloud is altostratus and the high cloud is cirrus. The dewpoint is 48°F. The barometer has fallen 1·8 millibars in the past 3 hours but is now rising. $\frac{2}{3}$ of the sky are covered at 600 feet by stratus cloud, $\frac{5}{8}$ at 2,500 feet by stratus, and $\frac{7}{8}$ at 10,000 feet by nimbostratus.

The international meteorological code is independent of language and the message given above, although composed by a meterologist thinking in English, is immediately intelligible to meteorologists who know no English.

The individual messages are collected at local centres and transmitted to national centres by teleprinter or radio. Europe is covered by a special meteorological telecommunications system with Bracknell, Paris, Moscow, and Frankfurt as its focal points, and similar arrangements exist in other continents. It is now true to say that the weather of the inhabited world can be ascertained at all meteorological offices within a short time of its occurrence. The volume of traffic on the meteorological communications network is immense – Bracknell handles about a million five-figure code groups every day.

Display and Manipulation

It is possible to display weather information in a variety of ways. In forecasting, the prime need is to form a synoptic view of the distribution of weather in space. The main working charts of the Central Forecasting Office are on a scale of 1 in 10 million and extend from the Great Lakes of North America to the Urals and from Spitsbergen to the Canaries. When greater detail is needed, as for instance with hourly observations, charts covering the British Isles on the scale of 1 in 3 million are used. Both surface and upper-air observations are also plotted on hemispherical charts.

The observations are entered on a 'station model', using red and black ink. The plotter uses a curious pen with two nibs, and it is a fascinating sight to watch an experienced assistant decoding and plotting observations at high speed, changing from one colour to another without the slightest pause. Entries relating to high clouds, visibility, dewpoint, and past weather are in red. Barometric change is in red if the barometer is lower than it was three hours previously, and in black otherwise. The remaining entries are in black, and all symbols and their relative positions are prescribed by an international scheme.

The oldest type of synoptic chart is that which displays pressure at mean sea-level. Given an adequate number of pressure readings and the knowledge that the wind direction obeys Buys Ballot's Law, it is not difficult to draw an *isobaric chart* of an unsophisticated type. It requires considerable practice and a good knowledge of theoretical meteorology to construct a chart in the modern idiom, complete with fronts and occlusions.

The isobaric chart has been the chief tool of the forecaster since the middle of the nineteenth century, but it is now supplemented by other kinds of charts. This is a consequence of the greater mass of upper-air data now available. The horizontal variation of pressure in the free atmosphere can be shown in two ways: by computing the pressure at definite heights above sea-level or by computing the heights at which pressure has certain standard values. The Meteorological Office, in common with most of the services of the world, has adopted the second method of representation as the more convenient, and the upper-air charts show the *contours* of the constant-pressure surfaces.

The standard pressures are 1,000, 850, 700, 500, 400, 300, 200, and 100 millibars. The *average* heights above sea-level of some of these surfaces are as follows:

PRESSURE mb	AVERAGE m.	HEIGHT ft
1,000	132	436
700	3,013	9,880
500	5,575	18,280
300	9,300	30,050
200	11,700	38,360
100	16,190	53,040

Thus the 500-millibar surface is about half-way between

sea-level and the tropopause over England, and the 200-millibar surface is just above the normal tropopause.

Contour lines are also isobars, so that the geostrophic wind blows along the contours as it does along the isobars in the more familiar kind of chart. Contour height is directly related to pressure at the surface, but by taking the difference between the heights of two constant-pressure surfaces we obtain a spatial representation of the mean temperature of the air between the surfaces. It is easily shown, by inverting the barometer-height equation (p. 16), that the *thickness* of the stratum between two surfaces of constant pressure is proportional to the mean temperature of the air in the layer. In addition to the contour maps, further charts are prepared showing the vertical difference, in metres, between the 1,000- and 500-millibar surfaces. The difference in pressure between any two isobaric surfaces measures the weight of air between them; cold air weighs more than warm air and so, whenever the temperature is low, the thickness is small. Equally, warm air is indicated by large values of thickness. Thickness charts thus exhibit 'highs' and 'lows' of mean temperature. The information available at any time is displayed to the forecaster in three ways: by the surface isobaric chart, by a sequence of contour charts showing the vertical undulations of the standard pressure surfaces, and by one or more thickness charts showing the horizontal variations in mean temperature. The geostrophic winds blow around the highs and lows of the contour charts and the thermal winds around the cold and warm centres of the thickness chart.

Analysis

The forecasting centre of a major meteorological service is always busy, because there is little time to spare between the receipt of the observations and the deadline for the issue of the forecasts. The Central Forecasting Office at Bracknell is a place of contrasts. The teleprinter reception rooms are unbearably noisy with the rattle of dozens of machines as the messages pour in from all parts of the world. The long pages of figures pass on an endless belt to the editorial room, where they are scrutinized and dispatched to the proper quarters. The forecasting office – a large well-lit room, equipped with desks with glass tops which can be illuminated from below, with walls and dividing screens hung with charts – is usually quiet. This room is never empty, day or night, workday or holiday, from one year's end to another.

The first step in the analysis is the preparation of the forecaster's working charts. The sea-level isobars and the 1,000-mb contours can be constructed directly from the observations as reported, but upper-air data are necessarily less accurate and less plentiful, especially over the Atlantic, and a modified procedure has to be employed to determine the contour and thickness patterns for the higher levels of the atmosphere. The sequence of chart preparation at the Central Forecasting Office is as follows:

(a) The current sea-level isobaric chart is drawn. The meteorologist engaged in this work has already a good idea of the distribution of pressure from his study of the preceding charts, and the current observations serve to adjust the details of the pattern to take account of the latest developments. Continuity is further ensured by superimposing the latest chart on the earlier one on an illuminated glass panel in the desk.

(b) The sea-level isobaric chart is converted into the 1,000-mb contour chart by assuming that 8 mb = 60 metres at 0°c. etc. The contours are drawn at 60 metre intervals and radio-sonde observations of the 1,000-mb heights are used wherever they are available. The 1,000-mb contour and the sea-level isobaric charts are, of course, very much alike.

(c) The 1,000-mb contours are copied on to the plotted 1,000–500-mb thickness chart, and the 1,000–500-mb thickness lines are drawn using the plotted thickness values (derived from radio-sonde reports) and the thermal winds (derived from radar-wind reports). The previous thickness charts are used as guides to ensure continuity.

(d) The 500-mb contour pattern can now be obtained, in theory, simply by drawing lines through the intersections of two families of curves, the 1,000-mb contours and the 1,000–500-mb thickness lines, a process known among British forecasters as 'gridding'. In practice, because of unavoidable errors in observations and smoothing, the process is by no means as straightforward as this, and adjustments are necessary to make the pattern agree with the winds, which forecasters consider to be more reliable, in general, than the reported heights.

The charts for the other standard pressure levels are constructed similarly. Their construction is far from automatic and at all stages there is need for scientific judgement. The subjective element cannot be entirely eliminated and a comparison of weather maps published by neighbouring European countries often reveals substantial differences, especially in the placing of fronts.

Prognosis

This brings us to the culminating point of the work, the preparation of the forecast. The team has now completed its analysis of the current pressure, temperature, and motion fields of the atmosphere up to very great heights and must begin to look into the future. Today, a weather forecast is almost always based on a *prebaratic*, a chart of sea-level isobars and fronts as the meteorologist thinks they will appear a definite time ahead, usually twenty-four hours. This is a 'time-machine' concept, like trying to write the head-lines of tomorrow's newspapers, the object of which is to make precise the reasons which lead to the forecast of weather, but no meteorologist expects the prebaratic to agree completely with the actual pressure pattern over the whole area. He is content with his work if the differences between the prebaratic and the actual chart are not significant in terms of weather.

The main steps in the production of the prebaratic are similar to those employed in constructing the charts of the current situation:

(a) The first approximation to the prebaratic is made from the series of recent sea-level, 500-mb contour, and thickness charts. In deciding on the shape of things to come the forecaster must bear in mind historical developments in the 500-mb pattern, such as the movements of the long (Rossby) waves and the positions of jet-streams. From the thickness charts he makes deductions concerning the movements and modifications of the major features and, following Sutcliffe's analysis (p. 103), will look for regions of cyclonic and anticyclonic development. Continuity with previous sea-level charts must be maintained and there are a number of semi-empirical rules to guide his imagination. Depressions are usually 'steered' along the thickness lines at about the speed of the thermal wind, but there is a feedback in that the thickness lines themselves are continually being modified by the moving depressions, especially if these are deepening. Warm fronts commonly move at about half or three-quarters of the geostrophic wind speed; cold fronts travel rather more rapidly. In addition, he must bear in mind the latest 'tendencies' or movements of the barometer, and he must be careful not to ignore the effects of topographical features, such as the Welsh mountains and the Scottish Highlands. All this calls for the memory and concentration of a bridge player.

(b) A pre-thickness chart is prepared for the 1,000–500-mb layer. Here again, there is some guidance from rules. Thickness lines, on the average, move at about two-thirds of the geostrophic wind component at right-angles to them, and there are limits of thickness for every month of the year which are not to be exceeded without good reason.

(c) The 500-mb contour forecast chart ('prontour') is prepared by gridding the 1,000-mb prontour, prepared from the prebaratic, with the pre-thickness lines. If this process indicates unlikely changes at the 500-mb level the prebaratic and pre-thickness charts must be reconsidered. This is the second approximation – time rarely permits a third!

The final stage is most critical. All the work to this point has been concerned with the pressure, temperature, and motion fields. With this material before him, and with one eye on the clock, the senior forecaster has now to 'put in the weather', that is, to decide for all regions of the British Isles what he is going to say about the sequence of precipitation, wind, cloud, frost, and fog during the next twenty-four hours. Even if the prebaratics and prontours were perfect, it does not follow that the weather forecast would be infallible. The relation between the pressure patterns and the weather is not unique, despite the inscriptions on household barometers, and much depends on the insight and experience of the forecaster.

Weather forecasting can never be simple, and, unlike most problems in physics, the task has to be completed in a limited period of time. A front on a chart may result in anything from a downpour of heavy rain to a mere thickening of cloud. Like the patterns of flow, fronts with their associated weather are always changing, either decaying or intensifying. The forecaster has to assess whether the air over particular areas is diverging and therefore sinking, with general 'drying out' and thinning of cloud, or whether it is converging, with consequent ascent of air and intensification of precipitation. The main difficulty lies in the fact that he is denied direct knowledge of the most pertinent factor, the vertical motion of the atmosphere, which must be deduced from other, more easily measured, elements.

Most of the weather we experience as in areas free from fronts, and much depends on the origin of the air masses, how they have changed *en route*, and how they are now being affected by heating from the ground, by cooling at night, and by the character of the surface over which they pass. These changes decide, for example, whether it will be showery, and how frequent and heavy the showers will be, whether fog may be expected and if so, how dense it is likely to be, and when it will form and clear. It is at this stage that the details of the temperature and humidity structure of the atmosphere have to be studied from the radio-sonde data plotted on thermodynamic diagrams, again chiefly as a means of assessing the slow but all important vertical movements of great masses of air over immense areas. Finally, the forecaster must never forget that almost all the meteorological elements are cross-linked and cannot be treated as independent variables. An over-estimate of cloud at night may lead to an underestimate of fog, or to ground frost being omitted from the forecast, and so on. It is natural that professional forecasters become impatient when they are advised that observations of the posture of cows or of the flight of gnats are likely to improve their predictions.

The preparation of a forecast of the kind published by the

press and by the broadcasting organizations is thus the result of intensive work by a team and not of a single man, although the ultimate responsibility rests with the senior forecaster. It is the custom of the Central Forecasting Office to hold a daily conference at which the current situation and the forecasts are reviewed, together with the additional charts prepared by the meteorologist who is responsible for the outlook beyond twenty-four hours. There is almost always a majority and a minority view, so great is the complexity of atmospheric motion and so large the number of possibilities.

Operational forecasting, that is, for specific purposes such as flights by aircraft, does not differ in principle from the process described above. The Central Forecasting Office provides guidance by circulating the main analysis, leaving the details to be filled in by the meteorologist responsible for the 'briefing' of the aircrew.

THE LANGUAGE OF FORECASTS

It is impossible to reproduce weather maps in a book of small page-size so as to show the detail which the forecaster needs for his work. Further, all forecasts are based not on one map but on a sequence, both for the surface and the upper air. For these reasons, specimen charts and forecasts are not given here. The reader, however, should now be in a position to appreciate that a forecast is not a flash of inspiration but a weighing-up of probabilities, calling for mature judgement at every stage. The final act is to express the conclusion in words, and this is in many ways the most difficult part of the whole process.

Forecasts for the general public, such as those put out by radio and the press, are difficult to compose because they have to cover many different areas and yet be limited to relatively few words. Such pronouncements must, to a large extent, be stereotyped; almost the only occasion when the

British forecaster can relax from the strict official style is
when he appears on the television screen or makes a broadcast on the sound-radio direct from his office. But in every
instance he must use a closely defined vocabulary whose
implications are not always obvious to non-meteorologists.
In ordinary English prose there is, for instance, no great
difference between 'showers', 'occasional rain', and 'intermittent rain', but for the meteorologist the first means that
there are patches of clear sky between the falls, the second
that there are brief falls from a continuously overcast sky,
and the third that there are relatively long periods of rain
with the sky continuing to be overcast in the intervals.

Temperature is described relative to the climatic or long-
term average for the region and time of year. A 'very hot'
day in summer means that the temperature is expected to
rise at least 7°c. above the average, 'hot' implies 6–7°c.
above, 'very warm', 4–5°c. above, and 'warm', 2–3°c.
above average. A forecast of 'normal temperature for the
time of year' means that the actual temperature is expected
to be within $\pm$ 1°c. of the climatic average – there is, of
course, no implication that the weather is in any way
'abnormal' when a day is warmer or colder than the
climatic average! Forecasts thus specify only bands of temperatures, except when attempts are made to indicate
extremes. Some imprecision is necessary when dealing with
large land areas over which surface temperatures may vary
considerably on account of topography and the nature of
the soil and its vegetation cover. The word 'frost' sometimes gives difficulty, for it can mean either a deposit of
frozen water or a condition of the air. In forecasts, 'frost'
means that the temperature of air at 4 feet above the surface
(the usual height of the louvred box or 'screen' that contains the instruments) is expected to fall below 0°c., and the
adjectives 'moderate', 'severe', and 'very severe' refer to
various combinations of wind speed and temperature that

are defined in official publications. The absence or presence, of an appreciable wind is very important in frosty weather, for a relatively small drop in temperature below 0°c. coupled with a strong wind can be more destructive to water pipes and car radiators than a much lower temperature in a calm. 'Ground frost', which means that the temperature measured by a small thermometer lying in the open just above a closely cut lawn is below 0°c., can occur even though the air temperature at 4 feet is above 0°c.

In forecasts of visibility it is necessary to use two concepts of 'fog'. In communications to aircraft, fog is defined, by international agreement, to be a condition of visibility less than 1,000 metres (1,100 yards). This stringent definition is necessitated by the high landing-speeds of modern aircraft. In forecasts prepared for the general public, including the motorist, fog implies visibility not exceeding 200 yards. Forecasts of fog should always be treated seriously because of its very patchy nature. The fact that the air is clear in the immediate neighbourhood of the listener does not necessarily mean that the forecast of fog is incorrect, for a few miles away traffic may be reduced to a crawl.

Examples of forecasts, with charts, are to be found in the official publication *Weather Map**, which also gives the standard vocabulary and the list of forecast regions.

THE ACCURACY OF FORECASTS

A question frequently put to the professional meteorologist is: 'How accurate are your forecasts?' The most likely answer is: 'Put in that general form, I cannot answer. You must be more specific. Are you interested in the reliability of predictions of rain, or gales, or fog, or what?' It is not difficult to make unequivocal statements about, say, the comparison between forecast and actual winds at 20,000 feet on

* Her Majesty's Stationery Office, 1956 (4th ed.).

regular air routes, but it is virtually impossible to assign any overall figure of merit to the forecasts made for the general public, and a little deliberation shows why this is so. A precise figure of merit (such as '80 per cent correct') requires that the relative importance of the various elements forecast be known in advance. One user may be interested in rain, another in wind. For some, the time of onset of rain may be more important than its intensity, for others only the total of rainfall in a period of twenty-four hours matters. Wind direction and speed may have equal significance for the yachtsman, and yet another class of user may be able to disregard direction and so to judge the forecast entirely on speed.

A general forecast is a literary composition and therefore open to more than one interpretation despite the attempts of meteorologists to define with great precision words which have a range of meaning in everyday speech. The natural variability of weather also makes checking difficult. A forecast that there will be frost in areas sheltered from the wind may be correct even if no frost was reported during the period because meteorological stations are not usually placed in sheltered areas. A forecast of the likelihood of thunder may have been justified even if no thunder was heard, and it would be unfair to assess such a forecast as a failure. All this does not mean that meteorologists are not very much alive to the desirability of checking their forecasts, and many schemes are in use, all of which, unfortunately, are open to criticism from one aspect or another. There is no internationally agreed system of assessing forecasts.

Errors in forecasts are frequently caused by faults in timing. It is not unusual for a front on a prebaratic to be as much as a hundred miles out of the true position. This may seem a large error and is undoubtedly serious for certain users in that the timing of the arrival of heavy rain is at

1a. Vice-Admiral Robert FitzRoy, first Director of the Meteorological Office

1b. Tornado at Peshawar

2a. Sounding balloon, old style. The Dines balloon meteorgraph about to be launched from Kew Observatory

2b. Sounding balloon, new style. A modern radio-sonde and radar-wind reflector being launched

3a. Lenticular lee-wave cloud in New Zealand

3b. Cumulus and cumulo-nimbus growing along sea-breeze front,
looking west, Brighton below, 18 June 1957

4a. Convection at work. Development of a large cumulus cloud

4b Convection at work. Hailstones at Tunbridge Wells, 6 August 1956

fault, but when account is taken of the scale of depressions, it is seen to be almost unavoidable. The forecaster has first to locate the front in a region in which observations are scarce, such as the Atlantic, and then to estimate the speed and direction of its movement. During the next twenty-four hours it may travel five or six hundred miles, or much less. Relatively small errors in the estimates can be cumulative, and a forecast of 'rain in the morning followed by better weather in the afternoon' may be falsified by the front being several hours late.

Climatological Means and Persistence

It seems to be generally believed that any system of forecasting which gives correct predictions more often than not, represents a significant advance on guessing. This is not necessarily true, for among other things, the value of the forecast depends on the wording of the statements, and it is here that the difference between 'precision' and 'accuracy' is important.

The statement that '12 is a prime number' is precise but inaccurate, and the statement that 'there are many thousands of prime numbers among the first ten million integers' is accurate but imprecise.*

It is not difficult to make imprecise but accurate statements in meteorology – a 'forecast' made in 1963 that it will rain sometime in June 1964 somewhere in the British Isles is very unlikely to be falsified, but it is so imprecise that it is valueless. It is possible to do much better by studying data from the past. Climatological records give mean temperatures over many years, and it is remarkable how rarely the annual mean departs greatly from the long-period average. (In the period 1920–49, only on two occasions did the annual mean temperature at Kew differ from the long-term average by more than 2°F.) Although individual months show much

* Actually there are 664,579 primes below 10,000,000.

larger departures from monthly climatic means, it is evident that the intelligent use of climatological statistics provides a very useful first approximation to a forecast, but one which is necessarily imprecise. The meteorologist must do better than simple climatological averages if he is to justify the claim that he has introduced some element of 'skill' into the forecasting process. Climatic data can reduce the chance of a gross error very considerably, and in all forecasts, the meteorologist consults the 'normals' for the period as routine practice.

There is, however, a second factor which is rather more subtle.

The condition of the atmosphere at any particular time is not independent of preceding conditions, although the dependence decreases sharply as the interval between events increases. The statement may be put more precisely thus: if the day (twenty-four hours) is regarded as the natural unit of time in synoptic meteorology, changes in weather are usually sufficiently slow for continuity to be apparent. Consider rainfall, one of the most variable of all meteorological elements. There seems to be no relation whatever between yearly totals; a dry year is as likely to be followed by a wet year as by another dry one. There is a slight but definite connexion between monthly totals – this reflects the occurrence of 'spells', such as those which occur in wet summers or dry springs. The interdependence is much more marked for daily observations and it is well established that the probability of rain on a given day is greater if rain fell on the preceding day. In meteorology this effect is called *persistence*; it amounts broadly to the statement that for certain meteorological elements a 'forecast' that simply repeats today's weather as tomorrow's is more often right than wrong in a long sequence.

The most persistent element among those normally forecast is temperature. This reflects the fact that adjustments for heat take place rather slowly in the atmosphere. Even the best synoptic forecasts of temperatures do not show a great improvement on persistence when judged by their respective root-mean-square deviations over a long period. The value of temperature forecasts lies instead in the undoubted ability of the synoptic method to allow substantial and abrupt changes of temperature (such as a thaw) and their timing, to be predicted.

In the Symon's Memorial Lecture for 1947 the British meteorologist E. Gold described a 'rather crude check' on the accuracy of Meteorological Office forecasts for S.E. England as broadcast at 5.55 p.m. by the B.B.C. during 1946. The check consisted of noting occasions when precipitation (rain, snow, drizzle, showers) was forecast, and when precipitation was reported at Kew Observatory during the period covered by the forecast. The results showed that the unqualified forecasts were correct on 90 per cent of the occasions. If the forecast was qualified as 'risk' or 'chance' precipitation was noted at Kew on 50 per cent of the occasions, and if no precipitation was forecast there was no precipitation on 74 per cent of the occasions. In other words, the synoptic-chart forecast of precipitation was right about four times out of five. In this test, persistence 'forecasts' (predicting precipitation when it was observed at Kew at the time for which the chart was plotted) would have been wrong four times out of five.

A more stringent test of the accuracy of the evening forecast was undertaken by the Meteorological Office for the period April 1955 to April 1957. This consisted in asking the meteorological officers at twelve official stations evenly distributed over the United Kingdom to compare the forecasts for their region with the elements recorded at their stations. The assessments were limited to the four most important elements, wind, weather, state of sky, and temperature, and were expressed on terms of an arbitrary numerical scale: 'good' = 2, 'indifferent' = 1, and 'bad' = 0.

The investigation showed that the daily score for all the test stations, averaged over 25 months, was 6·2 or 77 per cent of the possible. There was very little variation from month to month. The effect of persistence was evaluated very roughly at 7 stations over a period of 6 months. In this test the assessors were required to check the forecast 'The next 24 hours will have the same weather as the last 24 hours.' The result was as expected. In periods of settled weather the difference between the synoptic and 'persistence' forecasts was relatively small, but during periods marked by the passage of depressions the method of persistence failed badly. On the average, the persistence forecasts were about 25 per cent worse than synoptic forecasting, using the same system of scoring.

The results also showed that the forecasts for some stations were apparently less accurate than for others, but it would be wrong to conclude from this feature that it is more difficult to predict the weather in some parts of these islands than in others. The result more probably indicates that the assessing station was affected by some local topographical effect which could not be allowed for in a forecast made for a large area. It is often claimed that the local fishermen or shepherds are more to be trusted than the official forecasters; this is probably true for very short-period forecasts for a locality much influenced by orographical winds and clouds, and the sensible way to use the regional forecasts is to regard them as general statements to be combined as much as possible with local knowledge.

A 'forecast' which relies entirely on persistence, or is purely mechanical, such as making use of climatological statistics only, is said to exhibit zero 'skill'. Various arithmetical formulae, of differing degrees of complexity, have been devised to discover how much 'skill' is introduced by the conventional process of synoptic forecasting – in other words, how much better can the forecaster do than a machine which simply operates on the data by a rigid rule and exercises no judgement. All such formulae are open to criticism and it would be misleading to quote any of them here without going into their merits and faults in detail. At present, the most that can be said is that there is a significant amount of skill in synoptic forecasting, but the exact degree of skill introduced by the complicated techniques and the experience of the forecaster is still a matter of debate. The figures given above for Meteorological Office regional forecasts are probably as meaningful as any that can be produced today, but they are in no sense absolute.

Weather forecasting is like climbing Everest – the last thousand feet matter most. It is easy to be more often right than wrong, especially if the forecaster chooses to 'hedge', but to improve on the present high and consistent standard of useful forecasts is one of the most difficult tasks in science. No two situations are exactly the same, there is as yet little accepted theory on which the meteorologist can rely, and he is always racing the clock.

The ideal would be to have an infallible method of *calculating* the meteorological elements, like that the astronomer uses to calculate the apparent positions of stars. In the next chapter we shall examine how far this ideal is likely to be realized.

CHAPTER 6

Forecasting by Numbers

OF the many jests which meteorologists have to endure, one of the oldest and least deserved runs something like this: 'Astronomy grew out of astrology. Is it not time that meteorology became meteoronomy?' The reader who has followed the account of the activities of meteorologists in the preceding pages may now agree that the present-day science of the atmosphere bears little resemblance to the medieval nonsense which goes by the name of astrology, but he may still inquire why there is such a large difference between the reliability of astronomical and meteorological predictions. The question is reasonable and the answer, in a phrase, is that the two sciences deal with very different kinds of systems.

The predictions of the Astronomer Royal are published yearly in the *Nautical Almanac,* a title which reflects the fact that navigation still relies upon observations of the sun and the stars as the prime means of determining position on the earth. The volume contains a mass of information about easily verifiable matters such as the times of sunrise and sunset, the phases of the moon, the apparent positions of the fixed stars and certain special phenomena such as eclipses, all of which depend upon the configuration of an exceptionally stable system dominated by one great cohesive force, gravitational attraction. Events like eclipses can be predicted years ahead with complete confidence, if only for the reason that the failure of the predictions would require a change in the solar system of such magnitude that mankind would be unlikely to survive to be aware of it.

The meteorologist is concerned with the dynamical and physical properties of a not very stable system which is subject to the crossplay of several influences of about equal magnitude. He tries to predict the behaviour of a shallow layer of gas held by gravity to a rotating globe of irregular surface, heated by the sun, and disturbed by the redistribution and frequent change of phase of its water content. As a result the energy balance of the atmosphere, as we have seen, is not expressible in simple terms and since every meteorological element is linked with every other, the system is non-linear. The motions of the atmosphere are incredibly complicated compared with those of the sun and the planets, and at first sight it appears a foregone conclusion that any attempt to calculate coming changes in detail must be defeated by the sheer complexity of weather systems. This is certainly true today and may be so for all time, and the problem can be approached only by the study of hypothetical atmospheres in the hope that thereby it will be possible to produce results which are of real value in forecasting weather.

RICHARDSON'S DREAM

The Quaker mathematician Lewis Fry Richardson, who died in 1953, was a man of singularly original mind who made notable contributions to meteorology, pure mathematics, and the theory of politics.* In 1913 he became Superintendent of the Meteorological and Magnetic Observatory at Eskdalemuir, Dumfriesshire. Before this he had made some important advances in methods of solving differential equations by numerical approximations and between 1913 and 1919, at first in the 'bleak and humid solitude' of Eskdalemuir and afterwards, when serving with a Friends' Ambulance Unit in France, he used these ideas to formulate a scheme for what is now called 'numerical forecasting'.

The *Nautical Almanac*, to use Richardson's own phrase, is a

* See the account by E. Gold in *Obituary Notices of Fellows of the Royal Society*, 9, 1954.

'marvel of forecasting', a collection of extremely accurate predictions made many years before the events themselves. Richardson inquired if it were possible to produce, by mathematical methods alone, a like volume for the atmosphere. The account of conventional methods of forecasting given in the previous chapter shows that calculations play only a minor part in the production of the weather forecast, and that the real basis of the method is the partial recurrence of phenomena. Richardson suggested that it might be possible to devise 'a scheme of weather prediction which resembles the process by which the *Nautical Almanac* is produced in that it is founded upon differential equations'.

The visible result of this work, much of which was done in conditions of extreme discomfort during the war in France, was a famous book, *Weather Prediction by Numerical Process*, which was published by the Cambridge University Press in 1922. Although much has been learnt since, this book is still a valuable text on dynamical meteorology, and in 1922 was far ahead of its time. In its pages he stated his creed. No two dispositions of the heavenly bodies are exactly alike, and astronomers calculate their positions anew every year. Why, asked Richardson, should we expect any two weather maps to be alike, or even that like situations will be followed by the same sequence of weather? He goes on:

Perhaps some day in the dim future it will be possible to advance the computations faster than the weather advances and at a cost less than the saving to mankind due to the information gained. But that is a dream ...

To realize Richardson's dream requires affirmative answers to two major questions. First, is it possible to 'calculate the weather' in any realistic sense, and second, can the calculations be done in time for the forecasts to be of value? These are very difficult questions to answer with confidence even now, nearly forty years later, but with the knowledge gained in the intervening years we may at least discuss the problems realistically.

Is it possible to 'calculate the weather'? The atmosphere is a fluid and there is no reason to believe that it does not obey the ordinary laws of fluid motion. These laws are embodied in a set of non-linear partial differential equations to which must be added other equations expressing the conservation of matter and of energy. The motion of a fluid is completely determined by these equations when they are supplemented by what are known as the 'initial' and 'boundary' conditions of a specific problem. The unknowns of the equations are pressure, temperature, and velocity. If we could solve these simultaneous equations for any given initial and boundary conditions we should know exactly the motion of the air and the distribution of pressure and temperature at any time ahead, provided that extra-terrestrial influences, not included in the original specification, did not intervene to a significant extent.

Needless to say, there are some extremely formidable obstacles blocking the way. The non-linearity of the equations means that they cannot be solved by straightforward mathematical expressions. Further, there is no hope of knowing the exact state of the atmosphere over the globe at any instant (the 'initial condition') or precisely what happens on the boundaries (the surface of the earth and the fringe of the atmosphere) during the period of the forecast in sufficient detail. The ideal scheme is never likely to be realized. Richardson's aim was to obtain numerical solutions to simplified forms of the equations using plausible approximations to the initial conditions and the boundary values. But even if this can be done, there is still no hope that the results will be valid for indefinite periods ahead. It is impossible to produce a true almanac of the weather which gives the day-to-day sequence of rain, fog, cloud, and wind for any locality for the whole year. In the atmosphere, influences which are below the threshold of observation at one time may grow and become dominant in a few days, so that exact prediction of the details of the weather for long periods is in principle impossible. The calculations must be repeated at short intervals using fresh observations as the starting point.

The second question, whether the task can be completed in the short time available between the making of the observations and the deadline for the writing of the forecast, can be answered with greater confidence because of the invention of the high-speed electronic computer and its development into a reliable scientific tool in the last twenty years. Richardson, in a half humorous way, thought of the Meteorological Office of the future as occupying a building something like the Albert Hall (he may even have had designs on that massive relic of Victorian London), with human computors all around, in the boxes, stalls, and galleries and, in the centre, the chief mathematician. As information poured in from all parts of the world it would be fed out to the computors, every one of whom would have the dreary task of solving a small part of the exceedingly complicated equations over and over again. He estimated that to keep ahead of the weather of the world would require 64,000 trained computors, a figure which he rightly called 'staggering'. In 1922 most meteorologists regarded this aspect of Richardson's work as a proof by *reductio ad absurdum* that weather forecasts could not be produced by purely mathematical methods.

When human brains are replaced by electronic valves and relays, and human memories and books of mathematical tables by magnetic cores and cathode-ray tubes, the problem becomes feasible. As with all systems of forecasting, a mathematical method must begin with an analysis of the raw observations to produce the initial situation. There is no reason why this process should not be mechanized, and forecasting techniques of the future will almost certainly begin with observations fed into a computer direct from the tele-communications network. The machine can then construct the initial distribution by a process known as *objective analysis*. The second stage is the solution of the equations using the initial situation and certain prescribed boundary conditions. This leads to the construction of the prebaratic, a task which also can be performed by a machine, but the final step, the interpretation of the prebaratic in terms of weather still requires the human brain, at least at present.

Modern electronic digital computers are just fast enough to carry out these operations in time to produce short-range (twenty-four hours or less) forecasts for fairly large areas. Machines which are projected, but not yet built, may be fast enough to deal with weather on a hemispherical basis. The magnitude of the mathematical problem becomes evi-dent when it is realized that even the simplest of schemes requires that many millions of mathematical operations have to be done in less than an hour to produce a useful forecast for twenty-four hours for an area covering western Europe and the eastern part of the North Atlantic.

Richardson attempted one calculation of this kind, using a desk machine. He selected 10 May 1910 as a day on which observations were more plentiful than usual, and his forecast referred to the six hours from 0400 to 1000 GMT. The method of computation required the division of the atmos-phere by horizontal surfaces at steps of 200 millibars and into rectangles of sides about 200 kilometres. As a test of the method he computed, by immense labour, the change of surface pressure for an area in Germany.

The result was, in one sense, a complete failure. Although during the period of the forecast the barometer remained almost stationary in the selected area, the computations predicted a rise of 145 millibars in 6 hours. Changes of pressure of this magnitude are never approached even in the most active large-scale weather systems of the mid-latitudes, and Richardson's forecast was in error by two orders of magnitude at least. So gross, in fact, was the error that it must have required considerable courage to publish the details in a serious work of science.

We now know the basic reasons for the failure. In his use of the primitive equations of motion Richardson had to estimate the small vertical motion of the air as the difference of two large quantities, and unavoidable errors in the measurements had a disproportionate effect on his final result. What he had really evaluated was a large spurious convergence. In 1910 upper-air observations were few and not too accurate. Today, the widespread use of radio-sonde and radar-wind equipment enables a far more accurate picture of the upper air to be obtained, but the fundamental difficulty of assessing vertical motion is still with us.

The failure of the first mathematical forecast was relative, not absolute. In his pioneer work Richardson laid the foundations of the method and his approach was substantially correct. He is rightly regarded as the father of numerical forecasting and meteorology owes much to this extraordinary man who, true to the traditions of his sect, had the courage to publish the truth to the world, ludicrous though the result must have seemed to the meteorologists of his time.

MATHEMATICAL TECHNIQUES

Details of the various schemes put forward for forecasts based upon the equations of fluid motion have appeared, for the most part in scientific journals, since 1946. These papers, written at professional level, require considerable knowledge of higher mathematics and dynamical meteorology for their understanding. However, it is possible for the lay reader to follow the physical ideas which give purpose and direction to the work without a deep knowledge of mathematical physics, but it is not practicable to describe complicated mathematical procedures without bringing in some of the basis concepts of the calculus. Throughout the remainder of this chapter it will be assumed that the reader knows that the laws of physics are usually expressed as differential equations, and that approximate numerical solutions of these equations often can be found by the substitution of finite differences for infinitesimals, so that the differential equations are effectively replaced by algebraic equations, which can be dealt with by digital computers.

To make the processes of numerical forecasting clear to the reader it is necessary to explain the bases of the techniques which allow equations to be solved by machines.* The incorporation of mathematics into weather-forecasting has become possible, not because of a revolutionary discovery in hydrodynamics, but because suitable digital computers have been developed in the last decade. Conventional methods of forecasting require the meteorologist to form, at all stages, a mental picture of the physical processes at work in the atmosphere. The prebaratic is the embodiment of this picture in a chart. Because of the many variables a unique solution is not always possible, and all forecasts are, to a certain extent, subjective. It is unlikely that two forecasters, of supposedly equal skill and experience, working apart, would produce completely identical prebaratics from the same initial data. One of the aims of scientific meteorology has been to reduce the subjective element to a minimum, but a completely objective forecast is not, as yet, possible.

It is not difficult to devise an objective method of preparing prebaratics for very short periods, without bringing in elaborate mathematics or physical concepts, by the straightforward use of barometric 'tendencies'. Meteorological stations report the rate of change of surface pressure over the preceding three hours as a matter of routine. If these rates

* A 'popular' but more detailed description of the process is to be found in the author's *Mathematics in Action*, 2nd ed., London, 1957.

were used to compute the barometer readings for a few hours ahead, a prebaratic could be constructed on this basis alone. Such a method would be like that used in anti-aircraft gunnery. The 'predictor' attached to the gun uses observations of the flight of the aircraft to compute information which, in theory, ensures that the shell and the aircraft arrive at the same point in space simultaneously. The feasibility of the method depends on the fact that an aircraft cannot change height, direction, or speed instantaneously, so that any evasive action by the pilot takes an appreciable time to be effective. Similarly, the inertia of the atmosphere means that a barometric tendency must persist for a brief period, but the method would lead to impossible distributions of pressure if the extrapolations were continued indefinitely. As in the anti-aircraft problem, new observations would have to be used as soon as they became available.

This crude method is not used in professional forecasting, in which prebaratics are required for periods of twenty-four hours, but a somewhat similar procedure is followed in numerical forecasting where it is known as 'step-by-step integration'.

The process of step-by-step solution of a differential equation can be understood by considering the problem of calculating the trajectory of a projectile. The effect of the resistance of the air on the motion of a projectile depends upon the speed and shape of the body and upon air density, and cannot be expressed by a single mathematical function, but numerical values of the resistance have been tabulated from experiments for a wide range of conditions. The ballistician therefore cannot produce the solution of the equation of motion as a set of formulae giving the quantities the gunner needs, namely, the range, height, and velocity of the shell at any instant. To overcome this difficulty the trajectory is divided into a large number of small arcs corresponding to brief intervals of time, say one second, in the flight of the projectile. The air density, and the speed and direction of flight of the shell as it emerges from the muzzle are known, and the equation of motion is first solved approximately for these initial conditions. The result is good enough to give satisfactory approximations to the velocity and position of the shell at the end of an interval of one second. The equation is then solved again, using these data as the initial conditions, together with the appropriate value of the resistance as given in the tables. The trajectory has then been calculated to a point corresponding to 2 seconds time of flight and the process is continued until the calculated height becomes zero. The whole trajectory has then been calculated to a satisfactory degree of approximation.

A similar process is used in the meteorological problem. The aim of the mathematician is to ascertain the changes of pressure which result from certain physical processes specified by the differential equations. The starting point is a chart of pressure interpolated from observations made over a large area. With these initial data the equations allow the barometric tendency to be found approximately, but the result can be trusted only for a brief interval of time, say 1 hour. The pressures at all points of the area are then estimated from the calculated tendencies, the result being a 1-hour prebaratic which is used as the starting point for a new round of calculations. In this way a 2-hour prebaratic is obtained, and the process is continued until 24 hours of real time has been covered. The final result, the 24-hour prebaratic, can then be handed to a human forecaster to 'put in the weather'.

Basically, this was the method used by Richardson. It is especially well adapted for use with electronic digital computers because it consists of a large number of repetitions of the same type of calculation. A modern electronic digital computer is a complicated apparatus which works on simple principles. The essential elements are the *arithmetical unit* which performs certain elementary operations such as addition, subtraction, and multiplication, a *store*, or *memory*, and a *control system*. The machine cannot be adapted to use the subtle and sophisticated techniques which mathematicians have developed over centuries to solve differential equations, and can carry out only primitive operations, such as addition and multiplication, but at prodigious speed. In this way it can deal with problems that human beings despair of solving because of the labour and time involved. The first task of the mathematician who wishes to use such a machine is to arrange the process of solution as a series of elementary operations. This is called the *programme*, and the instructions to the machine are usually fed into the control unit by punched tape. It may take several months to prepare, encode, and check the programme for a forecasting system, but once this has been done the machine, apart from normal engineering maintenance, requires no further attention. The initial data are also fed into the machine by tapes and as the various steps in the calculation are completed the results are stored in the memory unit (which may take the form of an array of magnetic cores) to act as the initial data for the next stage in the calculation. The final result is usually printed by an electric typewriter in a form which allows the meteorologist to draw the prebaratic at once.

THE PHYSICS OF NUMERICAL WEATHER PREDICTION

Although the equations which govern the movements of the atmosphere are known, the application of high-speed computing to the problem of forecasting is not immediate. A computer is not a sausage machine which automatically converts raw data into predictions. The problem has to be 'set' from the physical standpoint, and for this it is necessary to bring in some of the knowledge gained in synoptic investigations.

The study of weather systems shows that there is a definite hierarchy of dynamical systems in the atmosphere, graded according to size. At the lower end of the scale are motions which are broadly classed as 'turbulent', and also fast-moving changes of pressure, such as sound and gravity waves. In turbulence near the surface of the earth, and in convective clouds, all three components of the velocity oscillations are about equal in magnitude. The disturbances which cause the oscillations, called 'eddies', are small compared with the depth of the troposphere, and in any realistic study of phenomena on this scale it is not possible to disregard vertical motion. Next in order of size come the larger systems which form thunderclouds and tornadoes, and here again vertical motion cannot be ignored.

The dynamical systems which dominate the short-period forecasting problem, the depressions and anticyclones of the temperate latitudes, have their own peculiar characteristics. Regarded as pressure waves, they are of very large amplitude and move slowly, and are thus very different from sound and gravity waves. As individual dynamical systems they possess the characteristic feature that their vertical motion is small compared with their horizontal motion, and their vertical acceleration is small compared with that due to gravity. Because of the small vertical acceleration the hydrostatic equation (p. 16) is very nearly satisfied and can be used in computing contour heights from radio-sonde ascents. The wind direction is very nearly parallel to the isobars (except near the ground) and the geostrophic balance is approximately satisfied, so that the horizontal acceleration is small compared with the Coriolis term, a fact which is used in deriving the formula for the geostrophic wind speed. Examination of weather charts also shows that, over periods of a day or two, large-scale systems behave as if all the thermal processes involved are adiabatic, that is, the air in them changes its temperature without heat being added or taken away.

These considerations suggest forcibly that, in the first instance, weather analysis by mathematics should be limited to the study of large-scale slowly moving systems of a two-dimensional type. At first sight this conclusion seems to be too restrictive. It is indeed obvious that such a method cannot possibly lead to highly accurate prebaratics because the complete neglect of vertical motion and of horizontal acceleration rules out most of the characteristic features of weather and excludes the development of the systems. Nor is it exactly true that air temperature does not change other than by changes of pressure. Further, the absence of friction from the equations means that there is no way in which energy can be dissipated.

What is left is a barotropic fluid in which temperature depends solely upon pressure and thus is constant over an isobaric surface. In such a hypothetical atmosphere there is no change of wind with height, so that the motion is the same at all levels and there is no convergence or divergence. Yet these limitations are not as crippling as they might appear at first sight. It has been pointed out that in a deep column of air convergence at the lower levels is nearly balanced by divergence above, and vice versa, so that the net or 'mathematical' divergence is small. This means that a simplified form of fluid dynamics can be hopefully applied to conditions at the so-called level of non-divergence, the 500-mb surface which lies at about 18,000 feet above sea-level. Here the motion of the air is less complicated than at the surface, and except in regions of very active development, the barotropic idealization is not too far removed from reality. At these heights, friction is not a first-order effect.

It remains to select a physical principle around which the dynamical scheme can be built. Clearly, this can be none other than the conservation of the vertical component of absolute vorticity. The work of Rossby and of Sutcliffe shows that vorticity is of prime importance in determining the motions of the air on the scale of the mid-latitude weather systems. Vorticity can be expressed in terms of the geostrophic wind and hence by the gradient of contour height. In the barotropic model, the geostrophic wind is the means whereby vorticity is transferred horizontally. The geostrophic wind has another useful property, in that it has been shown by the American mathematician J. G. Charney that when used in this fashion it acts as a 'filtering approximation' which removes fast-moving gravity waves from the calculations. Such waves have no discernible influence on weather, but they may introduce spurious effects in the calculations. Sound waves are removed by the assumption of incompressibility.

The problem is now set from the aspect of physics. It is supposed that initially there is a certain distribution of pressure and that this is known in fair detail over a limited area on the 500-mb surface. Except in regions near the centre of a depression, the contour lines are also streamlines, along which the air moves with the geostrophic speed. If the principle of conservation of absolute vorticity is admitted, how does the pattern change as the vorticity is moved about the area by the winds? The result should provide an approximation to the prebaratic for the upper air.

PRACTICAL NUMERICAL FORECASTING

The first step in a system of numerical forecasting is to derive the equations. In the account which follows this process is described in outline only for the simplest type of barotropic forecast, but the method illustrates certain principles which are common to all systems.

Let ζ be the relative vorticity of the motion and λ the term

$2\omega \sin \phi$, where ω is the constant angular velocity of the earth about its axis and ϕ is the latitude. The absolute vorticity η is then given by:

$$\eta = \zeta + \lambda$$

The conservation of absolute vorticity is expressed by the equation

$$\frac{\partial \eta}{\partial t} + \frac{u \partial \eta}{\partial x} + \frac{v \partial \eta}{\partial y} = 0$$

where u and v are the components of the velocity of the air along axes pointing east and north, respectively. The vertical component of the velocity is assumed to be zero. If the motion conforms to the geostrophic balance, u, v, and ζ are given in terms of the contour height h by the following equations:

$$u = -\frac{g}{\lambda} \frac{\partial h}{\partial y} \; ; \; v = \frac{g}{\lambda} \frac{\partial h}{\partial x}$$

$$\zeta = \frac{g}{\lambda} \left(\frac{\partial^2 h}{\partial x^2} + \frac{\partial^2 h}{\partial y^2} \right) = \frac{g}{\lambda} \nabla^2 (h)$$

where ∇^2, called the Laplacian operator, is mathematical shorthand for $\partial^2/\partial x^2 + \partial^2/\partial y^2$.

Some simple mathematical manipulation yields the *forecasting equation*:

$$\nabla^2 \left(\frac{\partial h}{\partial t} \right) = -\frac{u \partial \eta}{\partial x} - \frac{v \partial \eta}{\partial y}$$

This is a Poisson-type equation, in which the unknown quantity is $\frac{\partial h}{\partial t}$ the rate of change of contour height with time (or, in effect, the barometric tendency). When $\frac{\partial h}{\partial t}$ has been found by solving the forecasting equation, the value of h at a short time ahead (usually 1 hour) can be found and this process, repeated 24 times, gives a 24-hour prebaratic.

A large rectangular area of the earth's surface is now selected. For trial forecasts for the British Isles the area usually lies between 40° and 70°N. and 40°W. and 40°E. It thus covers a considerable part of the North Atlantic and Scandinavia and runs from the Mediterranean to Iceland. The area is divided, for the purpose of calculation, into a grid of rectangles of side (d) about 300 kilometres, with the lattice points numbered as in Fig. 26. From the observations

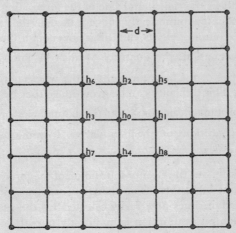

Fig. 26 – Lattice used in numerical forecasting

of contour height at the zero of time values of h are found at every one of the lattice points by interpolation. This array of contour heights, about 200 in all, constitutes the data for the initial situation.

The computer cannot differentiate but performs only certain simple operations such as addition. The differential coefficients are therefore replaced by finite differences, e.g.,

$$\frac{\partial h}{\partial x} \backsim \frac{h_2 - h_4}{2d}$$

$$\nabla^2(h) \backsim \frac{h_1 + h_2 + h_3 + h_4 - 4h_0}{d^2}$$

and so on. If d is reduced the approximations become more

exact, but the number of lattice points increases and the computation takes more time, and there is no point in reducing the grid spacing below a certain limit in a region, such as the North Atlantic, where observations are scarce.

At this point a difficulty enters. The scheme described above allows the right-hand side of the forecasting equation to be evaluated numerically at every stage in the calculation from the contour heights, but this is not enough. To solve the Poisson equation, the quantity $\frac{\partial h}{\partial t}$ must be known on the boundaries of the area throughout the whole period of the forecast. This difficulty can be overcome either by assuming some constant value for $\frac{\partial h}{\partial t}$ on the boundaries or by forecasting conditions on the boundaries. In some tests of the equation $\frac{\partial h}{\partial t}$ is given the arbitrary value zero, which means that throughout the twenty-four hours of the forecast period it is assumed that there is no change of atmospheric pressure along certain lines arbitrarily selected by the mathematician. Such an assumption is manifestly unreal, but fortunately the effects are not too serious. Provided that the period of the forecast is not too long, the deleterious influence of a false boundary condition will not extend too far into the interior of the rectangle. Mathematical forecasts of this type are therefore subject to the limitation that the results are applicable only near the centre of the selected area, and the restriction applies, but possibly with less force, even when the artificial condition of no change of barometric pressure along the boundaries is replaced by more realistic forecast changes. The boundary value difficulty is one reason why meteorologists need the fastest machines available, in order to push outwards the boundaries of their areas without increasing the grid spacing or making the time spent in calculation unacceptably long because of the increased number of lattice points.

The forecasting equation has to be solved at every lattice point twenty-four times in succession, which means over 4,000 solutions for a simple scheme of the kind described here. This process, without high-speed computers, would require several man-years. Richardson's original method, which made use of the primitive equations of motion, is still impracticable even when the fastest machines now available (1958) are used, but his scheme might be just possible if certain computers now in the design stage are successfully developed. There are, however, other difficulties in the use of the primitive equations yet to be overcome.

OTHER MODELS AND THE FUTURE

In a barotropic-model forecast, motion at one level is characteristic of motion at all levels. The real atmosphere is not barotropic but baroclinic, and a forecast at one level cannot be satisfactory for all levels. The 'one-parameter' model described above can be generalized to bring in thermal effects, and although the barotropic scheme has been used with fair success for routine upper-air forecasts in Sweden and elsewhere, it is customary to employ models which involve both contour height and thickness. The Sawyer-Bushby two-parameter system of mathematical forecasting now being investigated in the Meteorological Office requires the solution of two simultaneous partial-differential equations for the rates of change of contour height and thickness, respectively. The computations are again of the step-by-step integration type, but are naturally more complicated and take longer. The final result is a series of prebaratics for different levels in the atmosphere. Even more complicated models have been studied in America where numerical forecasting is now established on a routine basis to assist, but not to replace, conventional methods.

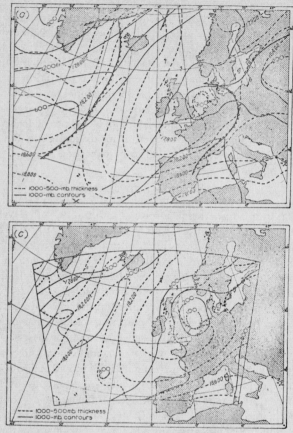

Fig. 27 – Example of numerical forecasting (after Pothecary and Bushby): (a) and (c) actual and computed surface charts; (b) and (d) actual and computed upper-air charts

The reader will naturally wish to know if the introduction of these complicated and expensive methods has brought about a marked improvement in the forecasting of weather.

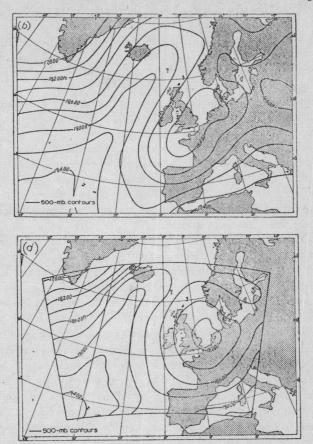

It is too early to give a definite answer, and at present comparisons are limited to prebaratics. Although some progress has been made in applying mathematics to predict rain areas, no scheme has yet been devised to deal with cloud amount, temperature, fog, and the other elements of weather in a quantitative manner. It seems to be generally accepted that, as yet, numerical forecasts are at their best at the 500-mb level, and that at these heights there is little to choose between man-made and machine-made predictions of the main air streams. At the surface the mathematical method has not yet reached the standard of the experienced human forecaster, a result which is to be expected since the equations omit terms which are important in the layers of air near the ground, and do not make adequate provision for topographical effects.

Fig. 27 shows typical prebaratics made with the Sawyer-Bushby two-parameter baroclinic model compared with the actual situation. There is a general measure of agreement between the pairs of charts, and the main features of the pressure distribution have been successfully forecast, but there are differences in detail.

The mathematical forecaster, when compared with an experienced 'conventional' forecaster, is like a bridge player who sticks slavishly to a system of bidding, compared with an expert player. When the cards are distributed 'normally', that is, according to the 'most probable' distribution on which all bridge systems are necessarily based, the bid, or forecast of the number of tricks made, is almost certain to be realized if the caller does not make serious errors in his play. If the distribution of cards is abnormal, such as all the opposing trumps in one hand, the strict system-bid may fail completely. The expert player generally realizes this from the bidding, and modifies his own calls accordingly. In meteorology, numerical forecasting for the upper air can rival or even surpass conventional forecasting when the atmosphere conforms fairly closely to the hypothetical fluid envisaged in the model, if only for the reason that the machine cannot forget or misapply any of the rules, but if the situation departs considerably from that postulated, the end result may be a disastrous forecast. Like the strict system-player, the mathematician cannot suddenly adapt his equations to deal with changed circumstances but must play out his hand to the end. For years to come, the meteorologist responsible for the forecasts must be allowed to accept or reject the mathematical results as his experience dictates.

The mathematical prediction of weather is still very much in its infancy, and there are many possibilities of improvement. The pure mathematics of the solving process is not yet entirely clear of suspicion, and gross errors may arise from this cause alone. The initial situation has to be constructed by analysis from observations which are liable to error and are always too few over the oceans, so that interpolation and extrapolation have to be pushed to extremes, and a relatively small error in the initial data may have serious effects on the final solution. Objective analysis may help here, but the real remedy may lie in the provision of more upper-air data, and this is bound to be costly. Finally, the equations, although formally correct, cannot take all the factors into account and at this stage in the study of dynamical meteorology it is difficult to be sure that the terms which are omitted are really of minor importance. The geostrophic wind, although an excellent approximation to the actual motion of the air, always blows along the isobars; weather, on the other hand, depends largely on cross-isobaric flow. It is for this reason that in recent years much effort has been devoted to establishing systems which are less dependent upon the geostrophic balance. Topographical effects, non-adiabatic heating, the effects of water-vapour – all these have yet to be incorporated into practical schemes, and a rich harvest awaits the mathematical physicist who is prepared to take the trouble to learn something of the trade of a meteorologist before he attempts to solve the problems of the atmosphere.

Numerical forecasting is undoubtedly the most exciting development that dynamical meteorology has yet seen. How far Richardson's dream can be realized is unknown, except that we may be quite sure that the almanac of the weather will never be printed. On the other hand, sufficient has been done already to show that meteorology is now becoming an exact science, the last and most difficult branch of classical physics to be brought to order as a mathematical discipline.

CHAPTER 7

Long-Range Forecasts

IN January 1901 the *Strand Magazine* published an article entitled 'Science in the New Century', containing the conjectures of eminent men of science on what might happen in their respective fields during the twentieth century – a hazardous venture, but the Victorian scientist was nothing if not confident. The century which had just closed had been remarkable for inventions and developments in every branch of science and engineering, and the reporter who collected the views had considerable doubts whether the coming years could possibly be as fruitful as those which had seen the coming of railways, steamships, motor cars, röntgen rays, and 'Marconi's messages'. The distinguished astronomer Sir Norman Lockyer had this to say of meteorology:

We can count upon the new century witnessing several most important achievements in the sphere of astronomy ... The first of these achievements will, I think, enable us by means of the spectra of sunspots to forecast famines in India and droughts in Australia, as well as other important changes, a long time in advance ... We shall also be able to predict, not only the time, but also the area and extent, of drought and famine, thus rendering it possible to take timely precautions.

There are, for us, many interesting features in this prophecy. The word 'meteorology' is not mentioned and the scientific study of the weather was evidently looked upon as a branch of astronomy. This is not remarkable when one considers the history of meteorology in Great Britain. After FitzRoy's death, and until Napier Shaw left Cambridge to become Director of the Meteorological Office in 1900, there had been little organized research into the science of the atmosphere in this country. In the nineteenth century the Meteorological Office, after a brilliant start, had lapsed into a dull appendage of a government department, and it was natural for a popular magazine to turn to an astronomer for news about progress in forecasting. In the next decade Shaw was to change all that and to place the Meteorological Office in the forefront of the national weather services of the world, largely by his insistence that meteorology is a serious science and that the forecasting of weather should be regarded, not as an empirical art, but as an application of physics.

In the language of present-day meteorology, Lockyer was claiming that the long-range forecasting problem was in sight of solution. He evidently believed that sunspots influence terrestrial weather to such an extent that they can be regarded as the primary cause of large fluctuations in climate, especially those that create famine by lack of rain. Sunspots are transient dark areas on the face of the Sun; they often occur as large groups of small spots that change into a single massive spot in a matter of weeks. Further, it is well established that the number of spots visible on the Sun varies periodically, with a maximum about every 11 years. Lockyer thought that by watching the variations in sunspots it would be possible to warn certain areas of the world that large deviations from the 'normal' weather were on their way. Unfortunately, this has proved to be a false hope. The search for the promised infallible relation between sunspots and weather was prosecuted with great diligence in the first quarter of this century, but without success. No connexion sufficiently reliable to be of value in forecasting weather has been found, and we still cannot predict serious droughts in India or in Australia, or indeed in any part of the world, a long time in advance.

Lockyer's statement, it should be noted, did not go as far as to suggest a physical process by which sunspot activity might affect rainfall. The method upon which he relied was *statistical*, that is, depended upon finding from past records a reliable relation between the variables without specifying the exact mechanism of cause and effect. This approach to the problem involves the mathematical technique known as *correlation*, which measures the amount of interdependence of the variables; it is widely used in meteorology and other sciences but is by no means the only weapon in the armoury of the meteorologist. Today, thanks chiefly to routine measurements of upper winds and temperatures and the invention of the high-speed computer, data are available in much greater quantity and can be analysed far more expeditiously than in the early years of this century, so that many lines of attack are now possible.

In the pages that follow, some of these methods are examined, but before this can be done it is necessary to explain how the long-range forecasting problem appears to the research worker today.

THE NATURE OF LONG-RANGE FORECASTS

For the professional meteorologist, a 'long-range' forecast of weather is one that refers to conditions in the atmosphere for a period greater than one week ahead. The actual period selected varies: usually it is one month (30 days) but some national services, notably the U.S. Weather Bureau, publish their 30-day 'Outlooks' at 15-day intervals, so that in effect the forecaster is allowed two shots at every fortnight in the year. As a rule, the 'official' forecasters do not go beyond a month, but others, outside the national services, sometimes attempt seasonal forecasts. The selection of the month for the period of the forecast does not imply a belief that changes in weather follow the lunar cycle, but simply reflects the prosaic fact that climatological data, for the most part, are tabulated on a monthly basis.

At present, and probably for a very long time to come, practical long-range weather forecasting deals only with the broad features of the weather that is expected to occur in a large region during the prescribed period. There is no attempt to predict the day-by-day sequence. Most meteorologists regard such an objective as unattainable, not only now but possibly for all time. A feature of the weather of a country like Britain is that although its climate (that is, averages of the meteorological elements taken over tens of years) changes only very slowly, it normally exhibits quite large short-period fluctuations. We are accustomed to speak of a notably 'warm' August or of a bitterly 'cold' January, meaning that for several weeks the average temperature in a region departed markedly from the climatic value. The long-range forecaster tries to foresee *anomalies* or deviations of the monthly-mean values of certain elements of weather (usually temperature, rainfall, and perhaps amounts of bright sunshine) from their established long-term or climatic values for the area considered, and he usually does so in terms of categories based upon the frequency of their occurrence in the past. An example from current U.S. Weather Bureau practice will make this clear.

CATEGORIES OF TEMPERATURE ANOMALIES

category	frequency of occurrence in past years
'much above' average	1 in 8
'above' average	1 in 4
average	1 in 4
'below' average	1 in 4
'much below' average	1 in 8

For rainfall, which is notoriously difficult to forecast, only three categories, 'light', 'moderate', and 'heavy', are used, each of which has the same frequency of occurrence (1 in 3) in the records. The categories refer to bands of values and not to single figures; for example, most long-range forecasters would regard a prediction of 'average' temperature as successful if, in the event, the monthly-mean values of temperature recorded at the main meteorological stations in the area all fell within, say, $\pm 1\,^{\circ}$C. of the climatic value.

These definitions impart a certain degree of precision to the forecasts – for example, a forecast of 'much above average' for the temperature of July means that the month is expected to be at least as warm as those which occurred, on the average, only once in eight years in the past. But the categories, when defined in this way, have an additional significance. They clearly indicate, in the right-hand column, the chance or probability of such deviations occurring in the future. This implies that if the categories were chosen at random (e.g., by picking slips of paper labelled 'much above' etc., from a hat) there would be some occasions when the 'forecast' so produced would be correct. The value of a system of long-range forecasting cannot be assessed simply by counting the number of correct predictions, but only as the result of a careful statistical examination of a long series of forecasts in order to ascertain if the results show a significant improvement on the 'chance' figure. The successful prediction of the nature of a single month, no matter how sensational, has no significance on its own, for it might be no more than a lucky guess. Apart from the intrinsic difficulties of the problem, one of the reasons why progress in long-range forecasting is so slow is that it necessarily takes several years to assess the value of a system.

The form of the forecast varies with the national service concerned. The U.S. Weather Bureau publishes twice monthly a four-page document containing information about the weather of the past month, with a written statement of the weather expected in the United States in the next 30 days and maps showing predicted departures of average temperature and rainfall from the climatic averages for the U.S.A. and the whole of the northern hemisphere during the same period. No specific forecast is made for the British Isles or any other country in Europe, but the northern hemisphere charts indicate, by lines and shading, areas in which temperature and rainfall are expected to fall into one or other of the categories described above. Other services, notably the French, attempt somewhat greater detail with an indication of the sequence, but in Britain the forecasts are confined to very general statements indicating that in the coming month the weather is expected to be warmer or colder, and wetter or drier, than the average, with some reference to weather types (e.g. whether conditions are likely to be predominantly cyclonic or anticyclonic).

We shall now look at the problem historically and technically, beginning with certain cherished but unfounded beliefs and ending with an outline of the modern approach.

THE MYTHOLOGY OF LONG-RANGE FORECASTS

The problem of long-range weather forecasts is now regarded as a proper subject for scientific investigation, but throughout the ages mankind has taken a somewhat different view. Inclement weather was long regarded as an indication of the displeasure of the gods, and good weather as a reward of virtue. With this went the peculiar myth of 'saint's day weather', that the weather experienced on a certain day indicates what is to follow. St Paul's Day (25 January) is one instance, but in Britain the most famous example is that of St Swithin's Day (15 July). Popular beliefs of this kind can easily be examined by reference to *A Century of London Weather*,* a compilation by the Meteorological Office that gives the summarized records of Greenwich Observatory from 1840 to 1870 and of Kew Observatory from 1871 to 1949. The St Swithin's Day myth

* Her Majesty's Stationery Office, 1932.

is based on the legend (which some authorities assert is a modern invention) that Swithin, Bishop of Winchester (d. 862) expressed a wish to be buried in the open, and that when his remains were to be moved into the cathedral on 15 July 971 he protested by sending rain for the next forty days. The St Swithin's Day forecast is that if rain falls on 15 July, some rain will fall in the same locality on every one of the next forty days, and that if no rain falls on 15 July, the next forty days will be dry. It is a curious fact that there are similar myths, but with different dates, in other European countries; in France it is Saint Médard (8 June), in Belgium Saint Godelieve (27 July), and in Germany the Seven Sleepers (27 June).

It is impossible to imagine any physical process whereby rain on a particular day of the year could ensure that the circulation over the British Isles would be such that rain would fall on the next forty days, but for those who are not disposed to accept this argument, the data of *A Century of London Weather* may be convincing. A period of 25 years, 1910–34, was chosen at random. During these years measurable rain fell at Kew on 15 July on 12 years and it was dry on the same date on 13 years – a satisfactory distribution of dry and wet days for a test of this kind.

Of the 40 days following the 12 wet St Swithin's Days, on the average 19 were wet and 21 were dry. Wet days outnumbered dry days in 6 years, dry days were more numerous in 5 years. In 1913, when it rained steadily from 4 a.m. to 7 p.m. on 15 July, only 9 of the following 40 days had measurable rain!

Following the 13 dry St Swithin's Days in the same period, there was an average of 20 dry days. In 7 years there were more dry days than wet days in the 40 days following 15 July, and the reverse was true in 6 of the 13 years. In 1924, when St Swithin's Day was dry and exceptionally sunny, there was rain on 3 out of 4 of the next 40 days.

The evidence against St Swithin as a long-range forecaster could hardly be stronger. The only conclusion to be reached is that the weather on 15 July in Britain is not related in any peculiar way to that of the following 40 days and there is no reason why this day, or any other, should be so favoured.

There are certain other beliefs about British weather that are widely held despite the fact that they have been proved on many occasions to be utterly unreliable. Their popularity probably depends on the fact that they are not really forecasts but fond hopes. After a cold winter it is natural to look forward to a warm spring or summer, and the expectation is nearly always justified by an appeal to the 'law of averages'. This 'law', which is unknown to science, seems to imply that natural processes are regulated by some kind of celestial audit which ensures that in the end there is an exact balance. A cricket captain who has lost the toss five times in succession may argue that 'by the law of averages' he is more likely than not to win on the sixth occasion, and the parents of a family of six daughters may believe that the seventh child is therefore almost certain to be a son. Some of the belief in this 'law' seems to rest on a wrong conception of the theory of probability, as exemplified by coin-tossing trials. In a long series of throws, the ratio of heads to tails should approach unity as the number of throws increases. If this is not so, the trials are held to be biased in some way or other. The statement, it should be noted, refers only to the final result and says nothing about the occurrence of long runs of heads or tails in the series. Further, in a long series of, say, ten tosses, the frequency of occurrence of a specified distribution, such as eight heads and two tails, can be expressed by a mathematical formula on the hypothesis that the events are random. The verification of the mathematical prediction is regarded as a proof that the coin was 'true' and that the method of tossing was unbiased. In mathematical language, the *probability* of getting, say, eight heads in ten tosses is about 4·4 per cent, that is, the event is expected to happen about once in twenty-three trials in a long sequence of ten tosses carried out in the same way. But this is not a method of forecasting the results of tossing coins but a criterion of the fairness of the experiment. With a true coin and unbiased tosses the most likely result is that there will be five heads, and the occurrence of an unusual score, such as eight heads, cannot possibly affect the next trial. All that happens is that the effect of the abnormal distribution on the final result grows less and less as the number of trials increases.

Consider now the popular belief that nature compensates for cold winters by warm springs or hot summers. It is possible to examine such statements objectively by making use of the data given in *A Century of London Weather*. The observations show that in general cold winters were followed by cold springs, and that exceptionally cold springs have been followed more frequently by cool or very cool summers than by warm summers. But there are many exceptions; the very warm summer of 1899, for example, was preceded by a bitterly cold spring.

The belief in the operation of the 'law of averages' in weather may seem to have some support in the fact that for a given locality the average temperature for the whole year does not vary greatly from year to year even over an interval as long as a century. This, of course, is simply another way of saying that climatic changes, if they exist, are very slow. A deficit in the mean temperature in winter may not be made up in the same year, or it may be made up by a few weeks of blazing sunshine in August or by a long mild autumn. On present knowledge, there is no way of telling in advance which will happen.

The 'law of averages' is not mentioned in treatises on statistical theory, and represents a crude form of anthropomorphism which has no place in modern science. At its best it is a truism, and at its worst a superstition which plays no part in the modern science of the atmosphere.

Contrary to popular belief, there is no evidence that animals, any more than man, are able by instinct to foretell the weather far ahead. Observations suggest that an animal reacts only to the state of the atmosphere in its immediate environment and is sensitive only to short-period changes, just as any sensible human being seeks cover when the sky grows dark with approaching rain clouds. There is also no truth in the belief that a plentiful crop of berries in autumn is a reliable sign of a hard winter.

A careful examination of the records has shown that no traditional saying or belief has any validity in long-range prediction. The only proverbial rules which stand up to examination are those which relate to short-range forecasts, but even these are not to be compared in reliability and accuracy with forecasts made from carefully analysed synoptic charts. Tomorrow's weather is usually over the Atlantic today, and it is straining the imagination to suppose that swallows and gnats in East Anglia have some instinct, denied to man, which allows them to know what is taking place west of Ireland. The 'official' forecast is by no means infallible, but it is a far better guide than seaweed.

We shall now leave the folklore aspects of weather prediction and look at some investigations of a scientific nature which, although they did not succeed in producing a reliable system of long-range forecasting, were clearly necessary in the effort to clarify the nature of transient climatic fluctuations.

PERIODICITIES AND WEATHER CYCLES

A periodic phenomenon is one that occurs in the same way at regular intervals. Primitive man must have recognized at an early stage that certain events, especially those connected with the movements of the heavenly bodies, recur regularly, and even today the timing of many religious celebrations, such as Easter, reflects the rhythm of the seasons which is the basis of all agriculture. The annual and diurnal variations of temperature are obvious to anyone, and it is therefore natural to look for 'cycles' of weather. If the Book of Genesis is to be regarded as history, Joseph won favour with Pharoah by the successful prediction of a 14-year cycle in Egypt, seven years of good harvests followed by seven lean years, but his interpretation of his ruler's dream would hardly find such ready acceptance today.

Meteorological records show that there is no exact periodicity in weather comparable with that which is familiar in astronomy. Although the general character of the weather in a particular year may resemble fairly closely that of another year, the agreement is never perfect. The nature of periodicities in weather has been well expressed by the British meteorologists C. E. P. Brooks and N. Carruthers. 'A rigid periodicity, such as those of the movements of heavenly bodies, postulates that at a certain time a certain thing must happen, i.e., a planet must be in its appointed place. A periodicity of the kind mostly found in meteorological data postulates merely that at a certain time there is a greater or lesser probability that something will happen than at some other time; in other words, the probability is periodic, rather than the event.'* Infallible forecasts based on periodicities are thus not to be expected, but it would be useful if the probabilities of, say, wet summers or cold winters could be determined well in advance, but even this is doubtful.

The simplest mathematical representation of periodicity is afforded by the circular functions, such as sines and cosines, which repeat their values at intervals of 180°. Natural

* *Handbook of Statistical Methods in Meteorology*, H.M.S.O., 1953.

phenomena usually require many sine or cosine functions, of different amplitudes, for their accurate representation. In this way a variable entity can be expressed by a fundamental wave and its harmonics, and the complete expression is called the *Fourier series* of the function. A crude representation of the diurnal change of temperature in the lower atmosphere can be obtained by the use of a single sine function plus a constant term, but for accurate work on the conduction of heat in the layers of air near the ground it is advisable to use at least three harmonics.

In statistics, the process of splitting a function into its constituent waves is known as *harmonic analysis*, and because of the importance of this work in tidal prediction and other branches of applied mathematics, machines called harmonic analysers have been in existence for a long time. The theory of Fourier series shows that any function, however irregular, can be approximated to any desired degree of accuracy by the use of sufficient harmonics, but this does not mean that the constituent waves necessarily represent genuine physical processes. Even if there are real periodicities in a series of observations, their length may not coincide with those of the harmonics, and the search for genuine periodicities necessitates the use of a yet more elaborate process known as *periodogram analysis*.

In 1890 E. Brückner, a Swiss meteorologist, concluded that the records of European weather, river heights, and floods from 1691 to 1870 indicated a 35-year period in rainfall. This period is usually called the Brückner cycle. There is better evidence for a 52-year cycle in British rainfall. The last peak of this cycle was in 1926, but the probability is never very large and predictions made with its aid are not very impressive.

The most important work on periodicities in weather is undoubtedly that of Sir David Brunt, who in 1925 carried out a long and detailed investigation into the variation of pressure, temperature, and rainfall at six widely separated European stations for which long sequences of reliable continuous observations exist. Brunt found a number of oscillations that are probably real (that is, arise from physical causes, not mathematical formalism), but these waves have periods such as 14, 19, 42 months, which cannot be related to known terrestrial or extra-terrestrial phenomena. The main conclusion reached by Brunt is that none of the periodicities found could be used, either singly or in combination, 'to calculate with any degree of confidence the value of the periodic variations for any future epoch', and this appears to dispose of the use of periodicities in long-range forecasting. Another major difficulty in the use of periodicities in forecasting is their lack of persistence. A periodicity may appear for a few tens of years and then vanish. Apart from annual and diurnal waves, the conclusion reached by Brooks and Carruthers (*op. cit.*) is that the oscillations calculated with so much labour are rarely, if ever, sufficiently persistent to be of use in prediction, and there we may leave the matter.

CORRELATION

The problem of long-range forecasting would be greatly simplified if the interdependence or association of large-scale climatological features, one of which precedes another, could be established. For example, it would be helpful if a reliable relation could be established between, say, the southward extension of the Arctic icefield in the winter and the general character of the following summer in Britain. To explain how the search for such relations has been carried out it is necessary here to interpolate some remarks on the meaning and use of 'correlation', since this particular statistical tool is used more than any other in studies of long-range forecasts.

It frequently happens in science that there are good reasons to suspect that changes in one quantity are influenced by changes in another, but the relation is either obscure or too complicated to be expressed as an equation. It also frequently happens that the quantity being examined depends, but to a lesser degree, on other variables as well. To take a simple but artificial example, it might happen that someone who was ignorant of the hydrostatic equation noticed that atmospheric pressure decreases regularly with height above sea-level. In a long series of observations he would find that when height is plotted against pressure the points fall very nearly on a smooth curve. He could then announce that 'height is correlated with pressure', but if he continued the investigation he would find that no matter how he succeeded in improving the accuracy of the pressure readings, he could never get complete agreement with trigonometrical determinations of height by the use of barometric readings alone. The reason, of course, is that the true relation is between height and density, and is strictly valid only when the atmosphere is not subject to vertical accelerations. This does not prevent pressure being a very useful measure of height, particularly if temperature 'corrections' are used, and in this instance the correlation between the two variables is of significance in practical matters.

In real problems, the situation is far more complicated, especially in biology. It is generally true, for example, that tall men weigh more than short men, but it is not possible to use this fact to predict the exact height of a man from his weight, no matter how accurately the latter quantity is measured. The statistician sums up such a situation by the statement that there is a correlation between the height and weight of men, and he uses a mathematical quantity called the *correlation coefficient* to measure the closeness of the relationship.

A correlation coefficient is a number derived from paired

data by a straightforward arithmetical process that does not involve any judgement. Suppose that when one variable is plotted against the other the points all lie near to a straight line. The magnitude of the correlation coefficient, which is defined so that its value always lies between ± 1, indicates how closely the points are grouped about the line. If the coefficient is positive, on the average the two variables increase together, and if negative, as one increases, the other decreases. The limits, $+1$ and -1, indicate perfect relationship, and the value 0, no relationship. The extreme values are never found in real problems, in which the points are always scattered about the line of best fit.

The apparent simplicity of the concept of correlation has led to much misunderstanding concerning its significance. The fact that an arithmetical operation applied to two sets of numbers leads to a coefficient different from zero gives no assurance that there is a causal relation between them. Any two sets of numbers which increase or decrease in a regular fashion must yield a non-zero coefficient of correlation, so that it is not difficult to find instances of high correlations between phenomena which common sense says cannot possibly be related causally. Thus there is a very high correlation (0.91) between the sale of radio reception licences and the number of mental defectives notified in this country between 1935 and 1946, and there are many other examples of nonsensical correlations quoted in text books of statistical theory. The problem of interpretation becomes much more serious in dealing with highly complex phenomena, such as the incidence of cancer. A brisk advertising campaign may cause a steady rise in the consumption of a certain food, and medical research may, during the same period, improve the methods of diagnosing a disease, so that the two variables, rate of the consumption of the food and number of cases of the disease notified per annum, show a steady increase over a period. Calculations would then indicate a high positive correlation, but this would be no proof that the disease is caused or even affected by eating a particular food.

These examples are quoted to show that in a science such as meteorology, with its many variables and still too few observations, there is a real danger of the research worker being led astray by the haphazard use of the correlation method. Fortunately, the skilled statistician is well aware of these perils and can safeguard himself, to some extent, from the danger of error. It would be out of place to enter into the details of such technical procedures in this book, but there are certain simple rules which can help the general reader to understand why meteorologists regard some relations as significant and others as not. First, before the correlation between the two variables is studied, it is essential to be assured that there are good reasons for the existence of a physical relationship. Second, it is necessary to guard against the temptation to attribute too great a significance to the value of the coefficient. A useful rule is as follows; if there is a real measure of interdependence between two simply distributed variables x and y, the fraction of the variation in y that can be attributed to changes in x is measured by the square of the coefficient of correlation. For example, if the correlation coefficient between x and y were found to be 0·5, the amount of change in y that is associated with changes in x is 0·25 or 25 per cent. The remainder of the variation in y is not to be explained by the hypothesis that 'x causes y'.

When two variables have been correlated, the result of the investigation is often expressed in a *regression equation*, or in graphical form as a line of regression, about which the points representing the individual observations are scattered in greater or less degree. Unless the correlation is very high, a forecast made by a regression equation may, on any single occasion, be very close or very much in error, and there is no way of telling in advance which is the more likely to happen. Weather forecasts are generally judged by their usefulness on specific occasions rather than by their average performance over a long period, and this explains why some meteorological forecasts, although based upon tolerably high correlation coefficients, are sometimes so wide of the mark as to excite derision. It is only when predicting averages over long periods that such statistical relations can be relied upon to give results significantly better than chance. For single predictions the result is often little better than that which would be obtained by drawing numbers from a hat.

In the problem of the relation between sunspots and weather, the possibility of a genuine cause-and-effect sequence cannot be denied. The sun is the only source of energy for the atmosphere and it is feasible that changes in the state of its surface could affect evaporation and convection and hence the entire sequence of weather, including rainfall. Lockyer was therefore justified in looking for a relation between sunspots and rainfall, but his confident assertion that in the succeeding fifty years this relation would be used for actual forecasting was founded on nothing more than optimism.

The relations between sunspot numbers and the three elements pressure, temperature, and rainfall have been thoroughly examined by Sir Gilbert Walker at 168 stations in all parts of the world. His results are as follows:

PRESSURE. Positive correlation at 39 stations, maximum value +0·36 in Brazil.

Negative correlation at 48 stations, maximum value —0·47 in South Africa.

TEMPERATURE. Positive correlation at 18 stations, maximum value +0·27 in New Zealand.

Negative correlation at 76 stations, maximum value —0·58 in Brazil.

RAINFALL. Positive correlation at 69 stations, maximum value +0·51 in Gambia.

Negative correlation at 81 stations, maximum value —0·50 in Canada.

These results are decisive in the problem of forecasting weather by sunspots alone. Even the largest of the coefficients means that at least two-thirds of the variation of the element is not accounted for by the hypothesis of sunspot activity as the cause. In no instance is the correlation high enough to allow forecasts to be made with confidence for single years, and for rainfall the element of chance remaining in a single prediction is not less than 85 per cent.

Weather travels from west to east, and it is a common belief that European weather follows that of America with a lag of some weeks. This belief has no foundation. Even if a depression travelled from New England directly across the Atlantic to the British Isles, it would undergo such changes on the way that the sequence of American weather would not be repeated here. An early December blizzard in New York is no indication of a white Christmas in London, and a July heat wave in Washington holds no promise of a blazing August in Britain. But there must be some relation between weather in different parts of the world although it is now generally accepted by meteorologists that, by themselves, such relations are not sufficiently precise to be of use in forecasting weather. The different climatic areas are linked by the general circulation, and any considerable departure from the average in any one region must have some effect elsewhere, but the atmosphere is so vast that it can absorb local irregularities without noticeable disturbance of the whole. Much time and energy was spent by meteorologists in the early years of this century in looking for such relationships. Sir Napier Shaw once drew attention to an apparent parallelism between the variation of the trade wind at St Helena and rainfall in southern England. An enterprising

London newspaper seized on this fact and for a time published 'forecasts' of rain in southern England based on the recorded winds at St Helena, but as any meteorologist could have said, the relation was too imprecise for the purpose, and the 'forecasts' were soon abandoned.

Many relations of this type have been investigated. Some of the more striking are as follows:

Variables	Correlation coefficient
Rainfall at Havana, May–October and rainfall in S.W. England in the following January to March	—0·54
Strength of trade winds in the N. Atlantic in August and temperature in Holland in the following winter	+0·76
Rainfall in Baltimore, January–March and at San Fernando, Spain for the same months	—0·57

These results were found in the early years of the present century, and although there are no reasons to question either the observations on which they were based or the actual calculations, it cannot be asserted that the same values of the correlation coefficient would be obtained if they were repeated using data for a later period. One of the difficulties in using the statistical method is that high correlations do not always persist, indicating that the original relation was, to some extent, accidental.

Among the best known investigations of this kind is that of Sir Gilbert Walker into the monsoon rainfall in India. Monsoon rain is a vital factor in Indian economy, and a reliable method for its prediction would be of considerable value. Walker found correlation coefficients of moderate size (not exceeding 0·5) between the rainfall in India in the monsoon period and certain elements of weather in other parts of the world earlier in the year, and he devised a forecasting equation which relates the departure of the monsoon rainfall in India from the long-term average to barometric pressure in South America in April and May, the subequatorial rainfall in May in Zanzibar and the Seychelles, the May snowfall in the Himalayas, and the average monsoon rainfall and pressure in India during the previous year. Even with such a complicated relation of a world-wide character the predictions are not very impressive, and the problem of long-range forecasts of Indian monsoon rainfall must be regarded as still unsolved.

MODERN TECHNIQUES

As examples of the present-day approach to the problem of long-range forecasting, we consider now the methods that are currently used by the United States Weather Bureau and by the Meteorological Office.

U.S. Weather Bureau

In the Extended Forecast Section of the Weather Bureau, medium-range (up to a week ahead) and long-range (30 days ahead) forecasts are produced under the direction of Jerome Namias, a distinguished American meteorologist who has spent much of his life studying the problem. The methods employed are complicated, but their underlying philosophy may be described briefly as follows. When a sequence of daily pressure charts covering a large area of the globe is averaged over a number of days to form a 'mean chart' for these days, the smaller and more transient features tend to disappear and some well-defined large-scale features emerge. The new features are held to be real dynamical entities and not fictions created by the processing of averaging, for they often persist and show recognizable continuity of movement from one mean chart to the next. Namias' work is based on the belief that the behaviour of such large slowly-moving features, which can be studied only when the smaller, more active systems have been removed by the process of averaging, furnishes a first approximation to the weather that lies ahead.

The characteristic feature of the American system is that attention is focused, for the most part, on mean charts for the 700-mb surface,* which on the average lies about 10,000 feet (3 km.) above sea-level. With the aid of a succession of such upper-air charts, some of which show variations in the height of the 700-mb surface and others departures of the actual heights from the average (climatic) height, a forecast chart is prepared to show the expected circumpolar mean flow pattern at about 10,000 feet, and the positions of the main troughs and ridges of the pressure field, in the northern hemisphere during the period. The weather expected at the earth's surface is deduced from this chart.

For the medium-range forecasts the charts are averaged over 5 days, the aim being to produce a 5-day mean chart centred 4 days ahead. For this, a 5-day mean chart centred on the day on which the forecast is being prepared is first constructed. Three days of this period are, of course, already known; for the remainder, considerable use is made of the 24- and 48-hour forecasts obtained by the mathematical methods described in the previous chapter. After this, a 5-day mean chart centred 2 days ahead is drawn, using the computed forecasts for 72 and 96 hours ahead, although at these ranges the accuracy of the mathematical predictions is somewhat dubious because of accumulated errors, and empirical corrections have to be introduced. Finally, by extrapolating from the sequence of 5-day mean charts, and by reconciling as far as possible the indications of various auxiliary methods that investigations have shown to be helpful, the forecaster produces the 5-day mean chart centred 4 days ahead. Forecasts of this kind, giving broad indications of the weather up to 6 days ahead, are prepared

* See p. 118.

three times weekly by the Extended Forecast Section.

These medium-range forecasts provide the data and much of the background for the genuine (30-day) long-range forecasts. The initial step here is to produce a mean upper-air chart, covering the next 30 days, from a sequence of such charts up to the present. Naturally, the methods employed are more subjective than those used in the construction of the medium-range charts; they make use of the trends shown in the shorter-range predictions as well as other indications that experience suggests have forecasting value, but only too often the aids available do not match the magnitude of the problem. It is here that individual skill and judgement based on long experience play the greatest part.

The broad pattern of weather at the surface is derived by objective methods from the forecast 30-day mean upper-air chart. There is, of course, no attempt to define the sequence of weather during the coming month, but only the extent to which the average temperature and rainfall for the period will differ from the climatic averages. The relations between the mean 700-mb chart and these anomalies have been derived statistically from past records, in considerable elaboration for North America and rather less precisely for other parts of the northern hemisphere.

Meteorological Office

Even today, the data that are used to prepare upper-air charts are insufficient to give a complete picture of the flow of the atmosphere over the northern hemisphere. A further difficulty for the long-range forecaster who wishes to use such charts is that reliable widespread upper-air records go back a mere twenty years. On the other hand, surface weather observations are much more complete and for some parts of the world go back for about two hundred years. In investigations into climatic changes and possible methods of long-range forecasting the variability of weather is so great that the advantages of very long series of observations are hardly to be overestimated – to find a British winter as severe as that of 1963 one has to return to the eighteenth century. In the Meteorological Office investigations into long-range forecasting, these considerations have prompted the use of surface charts, although it is well recognized that these cannot tell the whole story, and that the primary cause of weather changes must be sought in the strong flow of the upper air.

The method that has received the greatest attention is that of *analogues*, which involves a search of weather records to determine when the current situation was most closely paralleled in the same month in the past. The assumption is then made that the weather that occurred in the following month can serve as a guide to that of the near future. It is, of course, extremely unlikely that two years can be found with exactly the same sequences of weather in corresponding months all over the northern hemisphere, and in practice the problem of finding analogues has been brought within reasonable bounds by looking for years with broadly similar patterns of surface-temperature anomaly in the same months. International cooperation has made it possible to construct tolerably reliable charts showing the climatic distribution of surface temperature for every month of the year for most of the northern hemisphere; from these and the records of actual monthly-mean surface temperatures the Meteorological Office has built up a long series of charts showing monthly surface-temperature anomalies. On such charts there are distinct patterns of anomaly, with features that are sometimes remarkably persistent and often show a recognizable evolution. There is a close connexion between the anomaly patterns and features of the upper atmospheric flow, and hence with the general circulation of the atmosphere, whose perturbations are generally believed to be the root cause of short-period climate fluctuations. It is therefore not unreasonable to hope that similar temperature-anomaly patterns will be followed by similar sequences of weather for some time ahead.

The forecasting system consists of: (i) the construction, near the end of a month, of a surface-temperature anomaly chart covering a substantial part of the northern hemisphere; (ii) a search through the collection of historic anomaly charts to find the year or years in which the same month had much the same widespread distribution of temperature anomaly as the current month; (iii) a final selection of the best analogues by a comparison of weather sequences in the current and past months; and lastly, the production of the forecast from a study of the weather experienced in the following month in the selected analogue year or years.

This method has been used for several years by the Meteorological Office in the production of experimental monthly forecasts of temperature and rainfall for the British Isles. In practice the system is not always easy to operate, for really good analogues (that is, one or more years with good overall resemblances of pattern and consistent sequels in the weather of the succeeding month) are somewhat rare, perhaps not more than 3 or 4 a year. In the most recent development of this system use is made of mean thickness charts to study anomalies of temperature throughout the the lower half of the atmosphere.

Results

Long-range forecasts are necessarily imprecise and refer to large areas. As a result, it is very difficult to assess their accuracy. The crucial initial step is to select a number of representative meteorological stations in the area, so that their combined monthly-mean temperatures and rainfall totals will provide a fair picture of conditions in the area as a whole. When this has been done, there remains the difficult task of devising an objective method of comparing the results with those that would arise by chance.

During the memorable winter of 1963 the U.S. Weather Bureau 30-day 'Outlooks' were given much publicity in the British newspapers, but much of this was based upon a mis-understanding of the nature of these forecasts. The 'Out-looks' indicated only large areas in which the mean monthly temperatures and rainfall totals were expected to fall into prescribed categories within which it is possible to have large variations in the sequence of the weather. For example, a 'below average' mean temperature could be produced by rather cold weather persisting throughout the month, or by a very cold outbreak of brief duration followed by a succes-sion of rather warm days, or by a series of warm and cold alternations with the cold days outnumbering the warm. The forecast temperature-chart of the northern hemisphere issued in mid-January 1963 showed the southern part of the British Isles lying in a large area of 'much below average' temperature. This was interpreted by some newspapers as a prediction that the bitterly cold weather then prevailing would last for another 30 days – as it did – but this was going far be-yond the indications of the chart. No reputable forecaster would claim to be able to deduce the exact length of a spell of unusual weather and the forecast would have been no less successful if the very cold weather had lasted only 20 days.

The U.S. Weather Bureau has always been modest in its statements about the 30-day 'Outlooks'. An assessment of their performance for the U.S.A. has been published; this shows that for temperature the accuracy over a long period was somewhat higher than would be expected by chance, but for rainfall there was little improvement on the chance figure. The Meteorological Office experimental monthly forecasts were produced as part of a research programme and were not published. In the course of this investigation an examination of Kew temperatures showed that the period of 30 days is not the best choice for a long-range forecast, and that better results might have arisen if the American practice of overlapping 30-day forecasts issued every fortnight had been adõpted from the start. Despite this, a total of about 70 'one-shot' monthly forecasts produced in the course of the experiment showed a net positive score when assessed by a method in which 'chance' would have produced a score of zero, and completely wrong predictions a negative score. In other words, the forecasts were better than chance with a degree of success similar to that achieved by other systems.

As yet, no meteorological service has succeeded in making a real breakthrough in the problem but in many instances the forecasts, although far from infallible, are often sufficiently near the mark to provide better guidance than would have resulted from reliance upon climatological averages alone.

TOWARDS A FINAL SOLUTION?

In contrast to many other problems in science, it cannot yet be asserted that in time the long-range forecasting will be relegated to the class of 'solved problems'. It might be that the factors that determine the course of the weather a long time ahead are too randomly distributed, or cannot be observed in sufficient detail, to allow the problem to be solved in the usual sense of the word. At present, no service uses higher mathematics to any marked extent in the production of long-range forecasts, except in so far as statistical theory is involved. In short-range forecasting, dynamical methods are now being used increasingly, with marked success. There is no such clear-cut approach to long-range forecasting in sight.

We may, however, take heart by looking at the history of astronomy. Before Copernicus, Kepler, and Newton, complicated systems of curves derived from the circle were used to describe the motions of the planets. The studies of Copernicus and Kepler, that led to the overthrow of the geocentric model of the solar system and the discovery of elliptic orbits and the kinematical laws of planetary motion, were completed by the work of Newton on gravitational attraction and the theory of central orbits. Thereafter, it was only a matter of time before straightforward, if complicated, calculations could be used to predict infallibly the positions of the heavenly bodies. Perhaps the most spectacular triumph of mathematical astronomy was the prediction of the existence and orbit of the planet Neptune, from calculations based on observed perturbations in the orbit of Uranus, that led to the telescopic discovery of the planet.

The counterpart of this work in meteorology would be the establishment of a complete dynamical and thermodynamical theory of the general circulation of the atmosphere and its major perturbations. This is far more difficult than the problem of the solar system, but, if it could be solved, there is a distinct possibility that the long-range forecasting problem could at last be made amenable to mathematical treatment, and the subjective element that looms so large now could be eliminated.

The work of the American mathematician N. A. Phillips, which was briefly mentioned in Chapter 2, is an important step in this direction. Essentially, Phillips produced by mathematics a 'very long-range' forecast of the motion field of an atmosphere over a uniform rotating earth subject to irradiation by the sun in varying degree from the equator to the poles. The atmosphere was supposed initially to be at rest, and the final motion patterns produced by the solution of the hydrodynamical equations resemble those found in the actual general circulation, but not in detail, for Phillips' treatment did not take into account the influence of land and water distribution on the circulations. This is a most hopeful start.

This fundamental approach to the problem of climatic fluctuations is now being studied in many places, but as it involves the processing of large amounts of data and the use of very large computers (facilities for which are to be found only within the larger national meteorological services), progress is bound to be slow. It is perhaps no exaggeration to say that the dynamics and thermodynamics of the general circulation of the earth's atmosphere constitute the most difficult unsolved problem of classical applied mathematics.

In looking at the vast amount of work that has been done on the transient climatic fluctuations and their prediction, it is impossible not to admit that the record so far, of many whole or partial failures and some modest successes, is not encouraging. It is something of an act of faith on the part of meteorologists to continue the research. Yet the importance of the problem cannot be denied. Its solution would rank with the establishment of the calendar or of reliable tide-tables as a significant event in human history. For this reason man, and especially meteorologists, who are accustomed to disappointment, will not give up.

ODDITIES OF CLIMATE

As a relief, we conclude this chapter with brief accounts of some intriguing but unexplained features of our climate that have attracted attention.

Singularities

Although it may appear from the preceding pages that there is nothing in nature quite as irregular as weather, there is evidence that even in Britain not all types of weather are equally probable on any given day. Examination of the records suggest that periods of characteristic weather tend to occur on or about the same days in most years. Such spells of weather, called *singularities*, have been much studied in Germany.

In 1869 Alexander Buchan, a Scottish meteorologist,

announced that an examination of meteorological records for Scotland indicated certain well-marked 'periods' or 'spells' of characteristic weather, as follows:

WARM PERIODS	COLD PERIODS
12 – 15 July	7 – 14 February
12 – 15 August	11 – 14 April
3 – 14 December	9 – 14 May
	29 June – 4 July
	6 – 11 August
	6 – 13 November

This statement attracted little attention for the next half century until a proposal was made, in 1920, to fix Easter Sunday between 9 and 15 April, in one of the 'cold' spells. Since that time Buchan's periods have been great favourites with newspapers.

Buchan's spells are an early example of singularities. Their value for long-range forecasts is poor. An examination of London temperatures from 1841 to 1940 effectively disposes of the idea that there exists in our climate a marked tendency for these periods to be abnormally warm or cold for the season. The most that can be said is that cold spells tend to be more frequent in winter and warm spells in summer.*

Among the best known singularities in Britain are the following (based on Kew records):

CYCLONIC (CHANGEABLE)	ANTICYCLONIC (SETTLED)
24 Jan. – 1 Feb.	18 – 24 Jan.
26 Feb. – 9 Mar.	8 – 25 Feb.
24 Oct. – 13 Nov.	12 – 19 Mar.
24 Nov. – 14. Dec.	18 June – 6 July
25 Dec. – 1 Jan.†	1 – 17 Sept.
	15 – 21 Nov.
	18 – 24 Dec.

* These words were written on 16 August 1958, just at the end of what should have been a warm spell. The weather from 12 August to 15 August was cool and very wet over most of the country!

† Known as the 'post-Christmas stormy period'.

It cannot be too strongly emphasized that these are not forecasts in the accepted sense of the word, but the results of a search of past records. Their meaning is simply that, for example, over a considerable number of years, the occasions on which it was fine at Kew during the first fortnight of September outnumber those when the weather was of the changeable, rather wet, type. No great reliance can be placed on singularities as guides for holidays, for a singularity that has been well in evidence for some years may suddenly fail to appear. There is no way of telling in advance when this will happen. At Kew, September 10 has been dry more often than any other day in the year and could therefore be regarded as the best bet for an outdoor occasion in southern England, but there are no certain winners in meteorology!

The reader who would like to know more about this curious feature of our climate should consult the late C. E. P. Brooks' book *The English Climate** in which there is a full list of singularities thought to be significant for Britain.

Notable summers

In astronomy, the four seasons are simply the intervals between the solstices and the equinoxes, so that the astronomical summer lasts from 21 June to 22 September. There are no such rigid divisions in climatology, but for convenience meteorologists in this country define summer to be the three months June, July, and August. The British summer has always been an unfailing source of jests, and it is generally believed by foreigners (and also by not a few natives of these islands) that it consists of a succession of rainy days interspersed with brief periods of sunshine.

Yet not all summers in Britain are miserable for holiday-makers – for example, the glorious summer of 1959 showed

* English Universities Press, 1954.

British weather at its best – and it would be of considerable economic value to many sections of the community if a 'good' or a 'bad' summer could be foreseen well in advance. At present there is no reliable way of doing this. However, one strange fact concerning the incidence of notable summers from 1880 onwards has recently come to light.

There is no general agreement on what constitutes a 'good' summer but most people agree that an excessively cool, dull, wet season is 'bad'. In a scientific examination of the incidence of notable summers it is better to avoid such adjectives and to use only words that are descriptive of the physical state of the atmosphere. We need a single figure that expresses the general nature of the weather during the three months June, July, and August. In an article in the journal *Weather** Mr R. M. Poulter proposed an index for a summer that is really a weighted mean of the temperature, the hours of bright sunshine, and the total rainfall for the three months. High values of the index denote warm, bright, and dry summers, and low values, cool, wet, and dull summers. These indices were worked out for Kew Observatory for every summer from 1880 to 1961. If attention is concentrated only on exceptionally large and exceptionally small values of the index, the following 14 summers were notable in southern England.

'GOOD'	'BAD'
(*very warm, sunny, and dry*)	(*very cool, dull, and wet*)
1899	1888
1911	1890
1921	1903
1933	1912
1947	1920
1949	1954
1959	1956

There is no recognizable pattern in the sequences, but

* *Weather*, XVII, pp. 252–5 (August 1962).

it was pointed out by the present writer* that without exception, all the notably 'good' summers occurred in years of odd date and with the exception of 1903, all the notably 'bad' summers in years of even date. The year 1903 was very exceptional: it is by far the wettest year in the records for over a century, but for once there seems to be an explanation. In 1902 the volcano Mont Pelée (lat. 15N, long. 61W) burst into very violent eruption and it is generally accepted that the dust scattered high over the northern hemisphere was the main cause of the notable diminution of sunshine in Europe in 1903. Apart from this, the odd-and-even rule for notable summers has held for the last 80 years at least. It is difficult to examine earlier years for there are no Kew sunshine records before 1880.

A 'rule' of this kind inclines more to astrology than to genuine science and at once arouses suspicion that it is no more than a coincidence. Fortunately, the matter can be examined statistically to see if there is more in it than chance. If the indices are divided into two sets, greater and less than the mean value, respectively, there is, as would be expected, no significant relation between the numbering of the year and the nature of the summer, but if only those years with extreme values of the index are considered, the picture is rather different. For these years of notable summers, the odds against the relation between exceptionally 'good' summers and odd numbered years, and that between exceptionally 'bad' summers and even numbered years arising by chance is about 50 to 1, which is within the range generally considered to be 'significant' by statisticians. But this argument should not be regarded as conclusive, and a subtle point of statistical theory is involved.

If this strange fact is taken seriously, it appears that in southern Britain an odd-numbered year is unlikely to have

* *Weather*, XVII, p. 408 (December 1962) and ibid., XVIII, p. 95 (March 1963).

a notably cool, dull, and wet summer, and an even-numbered year is equally unlikely to have a notably warm, sunny, and dry summer. But in the absence of any kind of rational explanation, the odd-and-even rule of exceptional summers must be looked upon as a curiosity of climate and no more. It has certainly held for some 80 years, but it is impossible to say if it will do as well in the future.

Notable winters

There is no suggestion, in the records, of any coincidence between the date and the severity of the winter in Britain. The first half of this century was unusually free from very cold winters when compared with the nineteenth century; this applies especially to the periods 1896–1916 and 1948–62. The winter of 1963 was the worst experienced in this country for over 200 years, and on this ground such prolonged bitterly cold weather is not likely to recur this century. However, some climatologists believe that we are now at the end of a climatic fluctuation that came in with the turn of the century and resulted in an unusually low frequency of very severe winters. (There were, of course, some long cold winters in this period, for example 1947.) The evidence for this is, as yet, far from conclusive, but prudence suggests that for the next thirty or forty years those in authority in Britain should not rely on the experience of the last sixty years but should plan on an expectation of at least one severe winter in seven, or perhaps even more.

The subject of climatic change, with which the problem of long-range forecasting is inextricably bound up, is now receiving a great deal of attention, but it is gravely hampered by lack of reliable data, not only from the past but in our own time from the more remote parts of the earth and from the oceans. Although there are some indications that the gradual warming-up of the northern hemisphere that has been evident during the last hundred years is ceasing, there is no likelihood of our winters ever becoming as cold as those of Canada. Even so, the designers of our houses should take note of the fact that water sometimes freezes, even in Britain.

CHAPTER 8

Micrometeorology

ALTHOUGH living organisms have been found in the atmosphere up to very great heights, life is abundant only in a very shallow layer at the surface. We spend our lives at the bottom of the great ocean of air which envelops the earth and this is broadly true of all air-breathing creatures and plants. The detailed study of the lowest layer of the atmosphere, usually referred to as *micrometeorology*, is therefore of considerable economic importance. In addition, it presents problems of great scientific interest, differing considerably from those which occupy the attention of synopticians and climatologists, and it is in micrometeorology, if anywhere, that the mathematician really comes into his own.

Meteorological observations are made, for the most part, for synoptic meteorology and climatology, and for this reason, care is taken to ensure that they are representative of air masses over large areas. Thus the site is chosen to be, as far as possible, on flat land free from obstructions (airfields are particularly favoured) and temperature and humidity are usually measured at about 4 feet above the ground. If the thermometer is placed very near the ground, difficulties arise because at this level the temperature of the air is not only liable to large fluctuations, especially in hot weather, but also depends very much on whether the ground in the immediate vicinity is bare or covered with vegetation. These features, which are purely local, are not found to such a marked degree at 4 feet and above, where the temperature is much more representative of the air mass as a whole.

The climate into which a plant first emerges, which is also the normal habitat of small creatures, differs in many ways from that recorded at 4 feet. The climate of Lilliput is much more severe than that at the breathing level of a human, and even in temperate climates it is possible, in a single day, for the air within a fraction of an inch above the ground to pass from frost to almost tropical heat. But quite apart from these features, there is need to study the behaviour of the air near the surface in detail because of numerous matters of interest, such as the dispersal of smoke and of atmospheric pollution generally, on which meteorologists are often asked to advise. There is very little of weather forecasting in such studies. Instead, the micrometeorologist applies the normal methods of mathematical and experimental physics, and he is encouraged to do so because it is possible to measure the properties of the atmosphere at these levels with laboratory accuracy. He is, however, still limited by his inability to control the processes or to isolate different effects, as the laboratory worker can. He must observe events 'as they come', and not as he would like to arrange them, and he is never able entirely to separate an effect from others present at the same time.

THE WORLD OF MICROCLIMATES

When a meteorologist talks of the 'microclimate' of a locality he usually means the properties of the atmosphere within, at the most, two or three hundred feet above the ground, but he may equally well be referring to the world of ants and seedlings, whose atmosphere extends only a fraction of an inch above the surface. Within such layers the influence of the surface is dominant. The effect of the earth's rotation on the motion is no longer of prime importance, and the movements of the air are controlled by local pressure gradients which often bear little or no relation to the major gradients which are the concern of the synoptic meteorologist. The feature of the surface wind of which the micrometeorologist is most conscious is not, however, its magnitude and direction but its turbulence. Turbulence has already been mentioned in Chapter 3. For the synoptic meteorologist it represents a property of the wind which enters only indirectly into his analysis, except when he is forced to consider it in detail by its effects on aviation. In micrometeorology, nearly every problem involves the study of *diffusion*, the process by which a particular property spreads throughout the air. The process may be the scatter of particles of smoke, as in atmospheric pollution, or the removal of water-vapour from the surface, as in evaporation, or the spread of heat, as in convection, or even the diffusion of motion itself. Diffusion is brought about by the rapid random motion of molecules and also by the unsteadiness or turbulence of the wind, and in most cases of meteorological interest, the turbulent process dominates. The rapid irregular oscillations of wind speed and direction near the surface, which are regarded as 'noise' on the synoptic scale, are among the main objects of study of the micrometeorologist.

To see why this is so, we need only consider what the world would be like if there were no turbulence and only molecular diffusion were left. Physical systems would continue to behave in the same way, but at a much slower pace, for we could hardly imagine the disappearance of the Second Law of Thermodynamics, which in one form says that any physical system, if left to itself, must always change in the direction of greater disorder. A local high concentration of water-vapour or dust in the air always diffuses throughout the whole fluid, and never shrinks of its own accord into a smaller, more highly concentrated cloud. In this instance, as also in the case of heat, the diffusion is primarily brought about by the random motion of the molecules and this happens even when the air is at rest. It is also possible to make air move without turbulence ('laminar motion'), and in this instance molecular agitation alone causes diffusion, but the process is then very slow. If a little smoke is introduced into a vessel filled with air at rest, many hours will elapse before it spreads uniformly throughout the entire volume. Yet mixing of the air by a fan brings about the uniform state in a matter of minutes, by the motion not of single molecules but of large volumes of air. Turbulence acts in a similar way, and the irregular oscillations of the wind shown on instrumental records are evidence of the vigorous stirring of the atmosphere which takes place whenever the wind blows over the ground.

If such stirring did not take place, if fluids were such that turbulence could not occur and the particles in a stream of air always moved in a series of parallel planes, without intermingling, climate would be very different from what it is now. The atmosphere gets most of its heat from below, and in such an imaginary world the air would be intensely hot in daytime near the ground and very cold at the breathing level of a human being, for there would be no means by which heat could spread rapidly upwards. Evaporation would virtually cease because the film of saturated vapour over a water surface would not be rapidly removed, and human beings and animals could not congregate without fear of being poisoned by their own products. Obviously, many processes on which we depend for our existence would disappear with the turbulence, and the disorderly nature of natural motion must be regarded as essential condition for life as we know it now.

Micrometeorology is largely, but not entirely, the study of the diffusing action of the turbulent lower atmosphere, and this calls for advanced mathematical techniques and very specialized instrumentation. It is for this reason that micrometeorologists are nearly always mathematical physicists or experts in instrument design. Their work is nearer normal physics than normal meteorology, and in many ways, micrometeorology forms a bridge between the laboratory and the atmosphere as studied by the synoptician.

MOTION AND TEMPERATURE IN THE LOWER ATMOSPHERE

Fig. 28 shows a typical record of wind speed a few feet above the ground in twenty-four hours of clear summer weather.

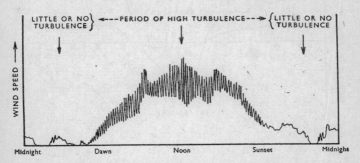

Fig. 28 – The diurnal variation of turbulence in clear weather

In the daylight hours the record is very irregular, with the oscillations starting soon after dawn and building up to a maximum about midday, after which they decrease and tend to die away about sunset. During the night the rapid oscillations are absent, and the general level of the wind is low, sometimes sinking to a calm. The turbulence of the wind near the surface thus exhibits a marked diurnal variation on clear weather. With overcast skies the oscillations usually show little change with the sun's altitude.

The fact that the unsteadiness of the wind is related to the elevation of the sun indicates that the temperature of the surface is involved, but this cannot be the whole story. A little reflection suggests that the control of turbulence must lie in the distribution of temperature with height in the surface layers. Fig. 29 shows what happens. If two registering thermometers are placed at different heights, one near the ground and the other a few feet above, it is found that from just after dawn to just before sunset, temperature falls rapidly with height in clear weather. This is known as the

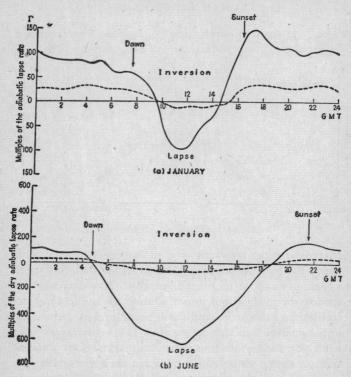

Fig. 29 – Diurnal variation of temperature gradient in clear weather
(after Best)

lapse period. From just before sunset to just after dawn the reverse occurs and temperature increases with height. This is the *inversion period*.

A comparison of Figs. 28 and 29 makes it clear that

turbulence rises to a maximum during the lapse period and sinks to a minimum during the inversion period.

These observations also point to the physical explanation of the variation of turbulence. During the lapse period, warm air lies underneath colder air, and any disturbance which causes the air to rise momentarily will be enhanced by the buoyancy of the lower levels. During the lapse period there is thus a continuous exchange of the lower air with the air above. Further, the motion of the air near the ground is slowed down by the frictional drag of the surface, and as the surface air rises it is replaced by faster moving air from above. On the anemometer record this is shown by a succession of oscillations, the gusts indicating the arrival of fast moving upper air at the anemometer head and lulls the upsurge of slow-moving surface air.

The inversion occurs when the ground is no longer heated by the sun and loses heat rapidly by radiation to space. Air in contact with the ground is chilled and becomes denser than the air above. There is now no longer any tendency for air to move in the vertical because of its buoyancy, for any volume of cold air displaced upwards is denser than its surroundings and tends to sink back, and any downward moving air is lighter than its surroundings and also tends to return to its original level. In these circumstances, turbulence is suppressed and the motion tends to become laminar, or nearly so.

These features of the surface wind are easily observed without the aid of instruments, especially by those who live in the country. On a clear summer day smoke from a wood fire is rapidly dispersed in all directions by the wind, which is then highly turbulent. As the sun sets, the inversion starts to build up from the ground and the oscillations die away. The supply of momentum from above is reduced and the wind speed falls near the surface. The result is that the smoke drifts in these compact sheets without noticeable mixing with the surrounding air. In these circumstances the motion of the air approaches the laminar state, but completely non-turbulent flow is never observed because of the oscillations generated by the roughness of the ground and by obstacles such as bushes and trees.

The study of the interaction of the temperature and motion fields of the lower atmosphere is still far from complete, but considerable knowledge of the properties of the air near the ground has now been acquired. Temperature gradients in the first hundred feet or so of the atmosphere have been measured systematically over many years and it is now known that they differ in order of magnitude from those found in the free atmosphere. As we have explained earlier (Chapter 3, p. 55), the equilibrium state of the atmosphere is one in which temperature falls with height at the adiabatic lapse-rate, approximately 1°C. for every hundred metres. The average lapse-rate in the free atmosphere is about two-thirds of this, but superadiabatic lapse-rates are not uncommon, especially in thundery weather. Such free-atmosphere superadiabatic lapse-rates are, however, never more than small multiples of the adiabatic lapse-rate. Near the ground the lapse-rate normally attains very high values in clear warm weather. For example, in the first foot of the atmosphere above a closely mown grass surface, lapse rates of hundreds of times the adiabatic value have been measured, and in the first inch a value of nearly two thousand times the adiabatic rate has been recorded in summer in this country.

The very rapid fall of temperature with height in the layers of air immediately adjacent to the ground reflects the very high temperatures which the surface of the ground can attain, even in a temperate climate like that of England. In southern England (Salisbury Plain) a tar-macadam road surface was found to reach a temperature of 60°C. on a hot summer day. At the same time a nearby sandy surface attained 54°C., and a closely cropped lawn 44°C. The highest surface temperatures are naturally to be found abroad; in Arizona, the temperature at 1 millimetre below the surface of the desert was found to be 71°C., so that the true surface temperature must have been far higher, and a surface temperature of 69°C. has been recorded in India. It is possible that surfaces exposed to a blazing tropical sun may reach temperatures approaching 90°C., which is not far below that of boiling water (100°C.). The mirage which is so frequently seen on roads in this country on a hot day as a pool of water is indicative of the very rapid fall of temperature with height in a shallow layer of air near the surface.

These examples illustrate the statement made earlier in this chapter, that the climate to which a seedling or a ground insect is exposed is completely different from that which is normally recorded at 4 feet above the ground. This fact is now well known to horticulturists and entomologists, but accurate data on the properties of the atmosphere very near the ground have only become available within the last thirty or forty years. A knowledge of microclimates is thus a matter of importance to workers in many fields.

THE STUDY OF ATMOSPHERIC TURBULENCE

Our knowledge of the turbulence of the lower atmosphere is still far from complete, but the foundations of the study were well laid in the second and third decades of this century, mainly as a result of the pioneer work of three men, Sir Geoffrey Taylor, L. F. Richardson, and the Austrian meteorologist Wilhelm Schmidt. The last-named published, in 1925, a classic of meteorology with the title *Der Massenaustausch in freier Luft und verwandte Erscheinungen* (Mass-exchange processes in free air and related phenomena). Taylor's famous paper of 1915 arose from a study of

Atlantic fogs, following the loss of the *Titanic* by collision with an iceberg. Richardson's highly original contributions were mainly published in the *Proceedings* and *Transactions of the Royal Society*, but there is a connected account of his early work in *Weather Prediction by Numerical Process.**

The main effect of turbulence, as we have said before, is to cause enhanced diffusion of matter, heat, and momentum. In a fluid at rest, or in laminar motion, diffusion is wholly caused by the restless motion of the molecules, and in calculation such effects can be described by use of certain physical constants called the molecular diffusivity, conductivity, and viscosity. These constants depend chiefly on the nature and temperature of the fluid, and their order of magnitude is 10^{-1} cm.^{2} sec.$^{-1}$. The earliest attempts to express the diffusing action of turbulence were based upon a supposed analogy between molecules and eddies, but it was found that meteorological phenomena required coefficients of the order of 10^3 or 10^4 cm.^{2} sec.$^{-1}$, that is, ten or a hundred thousand times greater than the molecular coefficients. These estimates were made in a variety of ways. Taylor and Schmidt studied the upwards transfer of heat from the sea surface or the ground, and Taylor used Dobson's observations of the wind structure over Salisbury Plain to determine frictional effects (and hence the eddy viscosity). In every instance the coefficients so calculated were of the same high order of magnitude, irrespective of the entity being transferred. Similar results were obtained by Schmidt.

At this stage it must have seemed to meteorologists that a difficult problem was well on the way to solution. To estimate the diffusing effects of turbulence all that had to be done was to repeat the familiar molecular diffusion calculations, but with much larger constants. However, it soon became evident that this view was untenable. Richardson, in the absence of better data, studied the diffusion of mass

* See Chapter 6.

from the results of a competition with toy balloons and from observations of the scatter of ash from a volcanic eruption, and found that to get agreement with the data, the coefficient of eddy diffusion had to be allowed to increase rapidly with distance from the origin of the particles. The same result emerged from Sir Nelson Johnson's analysis of the diffusion of gas and smoke at the Chemical Warfare Experimental Station, Porton, but these invaluable data were not released until after the Second World War and consequently were, for a long time, unknown to the scientific world at large.

A true physical constant cannot depend on the distance at the point of measurement from an origin arbitrarily fixed by man. The only conclusion to be drawn is that the theory is at fault and that no such 'constant' exists. To take a concrete example, consider what happens when gas is released continuously from a cylinder, or smoke is evolved by a generator on the ground, into a turbulent wind. The smoke is blown away by the wind in the form of a cone. By taking samples of the polluted atmosphere at known distances downward of the source, the rate of increase of the width of the plume and the rate of fall of concentration with distance can be determined. If the eddy diffusion coefficient (K) were truly constant, the well-established theory of diffusion from a continuous point-source shows that the width of the plume would increase as the square-root of the distance, and the concentration of gas or smoke in the atmosphere would decrease inversely as the distance from the source. The measurements by Johnson, on the other hand, showed that the width increased much more rapidly than the square-root of the distance (more like the three-quarter or seven-eighths power) and the concentration decreased more rapidly than the distance (more like the one and three-quarter power). Consequently, K had either to be increased as the distance from the source increased to make the theory fit the data, or else a new theory had to be found. The solution of the differential equation of diffusion with K constant evidently yielded formulae of an inappropriate functional form and a new approach was needed.

In 1922 Sir Geoffrey Taylor had published a paper on the problem of the random or drunkard's walk. In this problem it is supposed that a particle (or an inebriated citizen) moves in a series of unrelated steps, so that at any time a step may be in any direction. The problem is to determine the probability that after a given number of steps the particle will be at a certain distance from the starting point. This kind of movement occurs in *Brownian motion*, in which small particles in suspension in a fluid move in what appears to be a completely random fashion as a result of molecular impacts. Taylor considered the extended problem in which there is a variable correlation between the motion of a particle at one time and at some later time, and he succeeded in expressing the scatter of a cluster of particles after a given interval in terms of the double integral of the correlation coefficient.

Taylor's work did not attract much attention from workers in fluid mechanics at the time it was published. About 1930 the writer, who was then on the staff of the Department of Meteorology at Porton, made a careful statistical analysis of the observations on the cross-wind spread of smoke and gas. As a result he advanced the theory that a gas cloud diffuses initially mainly under the influence of small eddies, but that as time proceeds and the cloud grows larger, bigger and bigger eddies begin to dominate. Taylor's random-walk theorem offered a way of expressing this mathematically, by postulating that the coefficient of correlation between the initial and subsequent motion of a particle decreases at a definite rate as time proceeds. In this way, it proved possible to devise an explicit mathematical form for the correlation coefficient which contained one arbitrary constant which could be evaluated by observing the rate at which the wind varied with height. In effect, this meant assuming that momentum and mass are trans-ferred in the same way by turbulence.

With this method, it is possible to obtain expressions which involve only known constants or measurable meteoro-logical entities for the concentration of gas at any point in a cloud. These expressions are in tolerably good agree-ment with the observations. The method has also been used to calculate evaporation from a lake or from sat-urated ground, again with reasonably satisfactory res-ults.

Taylor's original work has since grown into the *statistical theory of turbulence*. At a slightly earlier date the German scientist L. Prandtl and his fellow workers at Göttingen produced the *mixing-length* theory, which had consider-able success in problems concerned with the drag, or resistance, offered by plates and pipes to turbulent flow. The latest development is an important extension of the statistical theory by the Russian mathematician A. N. Kolmogoroff.

It would be out of place in a book of this type to attempt to summarize all the developments of the past twenty years in the theory of turbulence which, under the urge of aero-dynamics, has now become the most important part of fluid motion theory. Considerable progress has also been made in the study of atmospheric turbulence, and data on the temperature and motion fields of the lower atmosphere, which once were rather rare and not too reliable, are now becoming increasingly accurate and plentiful. The basic problems of atmospheric turbulence, especially those re-lated to the conduction of heat, are still largely unsolved, but semi-empirical expressions now exist which are known to represent the facts of observation with tolerable accuracy in most cases of interest.

DIFFUSION AND EVAPORATION

The control of atmospheric pollution affords an excellent illustration of the practical application of the study of atmospheric turbulence. Pollution of the atmosphere by the products of combustion or by other noxious substances is an evil which humanity has tolerated far too long. The problem is now recognized as one of urgency, if only because of the increasing use of atomic energy. An excess of sulphurous products in the air has dire effects on health, but they are insignificant compared with the consequences for humanity of an unchecked release of radioactive matter. It is for these reasons that a close and detailed study of the spread of pollution from industrial stacks and other sources is a matter of extreme importance, for no industrial community, great or small, can hope to prevent entirely the escape of noxious matter into the air. There is no technical reason, however, why pollution should not be controlled, and the first step in any system of control is a quantitative study of the diffusion process involved.

The effluent from an industrial stack usually contains both particles and gases. Some of the particles may be large enough to possess an appreciable velocity of fall. These are deposited near the source. Very small particles and true gases are blown away by the wind and diffused by turbulence. In a well-designed industrial plant the large particles should be caught by grit arresters before they reach the orifice, but it is not as easy to get rid of very small particles and gases. In what follows, it is supposed that the effluent is either gaseous, or solid matter in such a finely divided form that gravitational settling may be disregarded.

The Stack Problem

When smoke or gas is emitted from a tall stack, it forms a long sinuous plume which stretches downwind, growing larger and less dense with increasing distance from the orifice. At first the plume behaves as if the ground were absent, but at greater distances downwind, when the cloud comes into contact with the ground, the influence of the surface makes itself felt. The ground presents an impermeable barrier to the plume, which quickly becomes asymmetrical, growing without hindrance upwards but retarded below. Mathematically, this is expressed by the statement that the part of the plume which is in contact with the ground is 'reflected'. This does not mean, of course, that the molecules of gas or particles or smoke literally rebound high into the atmosphere on hitting the ground, but simply that the effect of the impermeable surface can be represented in calculation by the assumption that for every particle which in theory crosses the line representing the ground, another fictitious particle crosses in the opposite direction. There is then no net transfer of matter across the line representing the ground.

The use of this mathematical device, known as the 'method of images', greatly simplifies the treatment of the problem. The result is shown in Fig. 30, in which the solid line indicates the concentration of the effluent (usually expressed in milligrams per cubic metre, or as 1 volume in so many

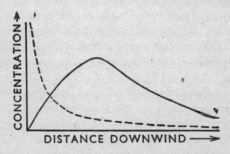

Fig. 30 – Concentrations from an elevated continuous source and a source at ground level

million) at ground level directly downward of the stack. The dotted line shows the decrease of concentration from a source situated on the ground.

It is seen that there is a marked difference in the behaviour of the clouds from the two sources as regards the variation of concentration with distance. If the source is at ground level, the cloud is 'reflected' at all points in its travel. The effect of the impermeable ground is simply to double everywhere the concentrations found in a cloud generated in an atmosphere without boundaries. In the cloud from the stack, however, the effect of the boundary varies with distance and the concentration at first rises fairly steeply to a maximum value and then slowly falls.

The calculations on which Fig. 30 are based, like all calculations in eddy diffusion, refer only to concentrations averaged over fairly long periods, never less than about 5 minutes and often longer. Such concentrations are usually measured by aspirating large volumes of the polluted air through bubblers or filters. No theory could possibly describe accurately the rapid individual variations of concentration which occur because of the incessant fluctuations of the wind and, for the purposes of physiology, such detail is unnecessary. Thus although the theoretical calculation shows that the concentration very near the foot of the stack is extremely small, it is quite possible, in practice, for an occasional eddy to blow the effluent downwards into this region. What the theory says is that if an average is taken over a long period of time, the effect of such random events is negligible.

The mathematical expressions show several points of interest. The maximum concentration experienced at ground level is directly proportional to the strength of the source and inversely proportional to the wind speed and to the square of the height of the chimney. The first result is to be expected on common-sense grounds and the second shows that the wind dilutes the cloud by spreading its contents through greater and greater volumes as the speed increases. The result that the maximum concentration at ground varies inversely as the square of the stack height, however, is not immediately obvious. It makes precise the importance of tall stacks in reducing the level of pollution – thus raising the orifice from 30 feet to 100 feet above the ground would decrease the maximum concentration of the effluent at ground level by a factor of nearly 10. Another effect of raising the orifice is to make the point of maximum concentration recede further downwind, the distance from the foot of the stack being approximately proportional to the height of the stack.

Hot Plumes

The calculations quoted above apply only when the effluent has the same density as the ambient air. Most chimneys emit hot gases or smokes, and this fact has very important repercussions on the concentrations experienced at ground level. Hot smoke rises because of its reduced density compared with the surrounding air and this effectively increases the height of the orifice. The calculation of the behaviour of a jet of heated gas in a horizontal wind is difficult and the problem has not yet been completely solved, but approximate impressions have been found which are of considerable use in estimating the beneficial effects of keeping the gases at the highest possible temperature.

The necessity to conserve heat as much as possible is well illustrated by experience with a smelter at Murray, Utah, U.S.A. Although a fairly tall stack was in use, the sulphur dioxide emitted caused considerable havoc among growing crops in the neighbouring countryside. The first attempt to reduce the nuisance, by blowing in cold air at the foot of the stack by a fan, was singularly ill advised. The result was an increase in the concentrations measured downwind of the smelter, because the gases, being considerably chilled by the cold air, did not rise as high as before. An increase in the height of the stack brought about a considerable improvement but the concentrations were not reduced to an acceptably low level until the incoming gases were heated to a high temperature. The golden rule for the designers of industrial plant is this – keep both the stack and the temperature of the effluent as high as possible.

The main danger from atmospheric pollution arises when an inversion is present in the lower atmosphere. The theories of diffusion which have been developed so far refer, for the most part, to conditions in which there are no marked vertical gradients of temperature. The extension of these theories to atmosphere dominated by large lapse-rates or large inversions is difficult, and the study of turbulence in a stratified atmosphere is one of the main preoccupations of the present-day micrometeorologist.

Evaporation

The process by which water is removed from a surface by an air stream is known as evaporation, and every housewife knows that clothes dry more rapidly when the air is warm and dry and there is a fresh or strong wind. These facts are easily interpreted in terms of physics. The fact that the air is warm and dry means that the *saturation deficit*, or the difference between the actual pressure of the water-vapour in the air and its saturation value, is high. The brisk wind means that the water-vapour molecules are rapidly swept away from the surface of the clothes and, finally, the warmth of the air also ensures that the water molecules held in the fibre of the cloth have greater energy with which to escape. As a first step towards a theory of evaporation we may therefore say that the rate of evaporation depends directly on the saturation deficit and the speed of the wind, a statement sometimes known as *Dalton's law*.

A more detailed examination of the problem, however, shows that the matter is more complicated than this. First, we must distinguish clearly between two problems – evaporation from a surface of limited area, such as a lake, and evaporation from an unlimited area, such as an ocean. In the first problem it is supposed that air, whose water-vapour content is below saturation, moves from dry land over a water surface. As it passes over the water it forms a blanket of vapour whose depth increases with distance from the shore. Evaporation occurs because the molecules of vapour escaping from the water surface are continually swept away, and the problem is to calculate the rate at which the lake loses water to the air in terms of measurable meteorological entities.

The problem was solved in 1934 by the present writer, in terms of the statistical diffusion theory, for the case in which the transport of water-vapour across-wind is neglected, i.e. the lake is supposed to be very long across-wind compared with its length downwind. It was found that evaporation from a strip distant x from the upwind shore in a wind of speed v was given by:

$$\text{evaporation} = (\text{constant}) \times (\text{saturation deficit}) \, x^{\frac{3}{3}} v^{\frac{4}{3}}$$

so that the total evaporation is not simply proportional to the area exposed, as might have been expected. This effect arises from the gradual thickening of the vapour blanket with distance downwind. The expression has been compared with experimental results from wind tunnels and found to be satisfactory. The extended problem of evaporation from an area which is not long across-wind is extremely difficult and has not yet been fully solved.

In the finite-area problem, the rate of evaporation depends, *inter alia*, on the distance of the area considered from the upwind edge of the water. In the infinite-area problem, evaporation must be the same at all points. Formulae have been devised which allow the rate of evaporation from a large area to be found from measurements of the humidity and wind speed at two positions above the surface, one fairly near the ground and the other some metres higher.

Methods of this kind, which call for the use of specially designed sensitive anemometers and hygrometers (usually of the electrical type), are used only in experiments in which the highest possible accuracy is required. For the purposes of agriculture and water engineering such meticulous accuracy is often unnecessary. What is required for these purposes is a reliable estimate of water losses from very large areas for which only broad climatological data are available.

The procedure adopted in making such estimates is known as the *energy-balance method*. The incoming radiation from the sun, direct or diffuse, is balanced by the reflected solar radiation, the upward stream of long-wave (infra-red) radiation from the surface and from the vegetation, convection and conduction of heat from the surface upward, the downward flow of heat into the soil, and the heat used in evaporation. Most of these quantities can be estimated directly from climatological records; the chief uncertainty lies in the estimation of heat loss by convection (turbulence) and conduction into the air. When all the quantities except the heat used in evaporation have been estimated, the difference between the incoming radiation and the total gives the energy absorbed by the evaporation process and thus leads directly to the amount of water-vapour taken into the air.

This approach, which had been elaborated in this country by H. L. Penman and in America by C. W. Thornthwaite, has proved extremely useful to agriculturists. The average loss of water from soil and plants (sometimes called evapotranspiration) has been calculated by the Meteorological Office for most places in Great Britain for which data are available. Such estimates have a two-fold use: first, they help to determine the water requirements of a crop and second, they indicate the irrigation needs of a region.*

Even a country like Britain, which traditionally gets more rain than it needs, may be forced to conserve its water supplies in the future because of the rapidly increasing demands of the populace and of industry. The importance of a reliable assessment of the water balance is obvious, and in the account, rainfall, evaporation, and run-off are the major items. The first two are the concern of the meteorologist, so that studies of the turbulent exchange-processes which cause evaporation are of more than academic interest.

THE TRANSFER OF HEAT IN THE LOWER ATMOSPHERE

On a cloudless day, a registering thermometer at the usual height of 4 feet above the ground shows that the temperature of the air begins to rise soon after dawn, attains a rather ill-defined maximum value about 2 or $2\frac{1}{2}$ hours after local noon, and thereafter decreases. During the hours of darkness the variation is somewhat different, the minimum temperature being reached just before dawn. If broken cloud is present, the temperature record is usually very irregular.

The physical processes involved are complicated and not independent of each other. The solar beam heats the surface of the ground. Some of the heat is conducted into the soil, some is used up in evaporation and much passes to the air by conduction and convection. In addition, the ground loses heat by long-wave radiation, especially on a clear night.

The details of the balance sheet vary considerably with the nature of the surface, and accurate figures are available only for a few sites and then over limited periods. On a clear day in spring in southern England Dr F. Pasquill found that at noon, of the incoming solar energy about 17 per cent was

* See Ministry of Agriculture, Fisheries and Food *Technical Bulletin* No. 4 and *Farming Weather* by L. P. Smith, London (Nelson & Sons), 1958

reflected back to space, 25 per cent was emitted by the ground as long-wave (infra-red) radiation, 15 per cent was absorbed by the ground, 15 per cent used up in evaporation, and the remainder of the incoming energy, about 28 per cent, was transferred to the air by turbulence. In Finland, Homen found that a rocky surface absorbed over 40 per cent of the energy of the incoming beam and that about 33 per cent was transferred to the atmosphere by turbulence during an August day. On the same occasion a sandy heath gave about 40 per cent of the incoming energy to the air by turbulence but a nearby meadow only about 18 per cent.

The shape of the diurnal temperature curve varies with height, being very sharply peaked at the surface, growing flatter with height. The time of maximum temperature also changes with height. On the surface itself, the maximum temperature is reached about 1 hour after local noon, when the solar radiation has passed its peak. This is because the maximum surface temperature is attained when the flow of heat into the soil exactly balances the outward flow, and not when the energy income is greatest. At Porton, Salisbury Plain, during a period of clear spring weather the following times of maximum temperatures were found:

Height (cm.)	0	2·5	30	120	710	1710
Time of maximum temperature (GMT)	1.17	1.48	2.05	2.30	2.45	3.00 p.m.

Thus at the normal height of observation, 120 cm., the air does not reach its maximum temperature until about 2.30 in the afternoon. At Leafield, Oxfordshire, observations on a radio tower nearly 90 metres high showed that in June the air at that level was hottest at about 5.20 p.m.

The diurnal variation of temperature is regarded, mathematically, as the passage of a wave of heat which starts at the surface and is propogated upwards by turbulence. As this wave travels through the atmosphere its amplitude decreases and its phase, as shown by the time of maximum temperature, increases. There is a well-developed mathematical theory for calculating the conductivity of the air from observations of the amplitude and phase of such waves. When applied to the lower atmosphere this theory shows that if the eddy conductivity (K) is treated as constant, values of the order of 10^3 to 10^4 cm.^{2} sec.^{1} are required by the observations. This again indicates the enormous difference in scale between eddy and molecular transfer processes, for the molecular conductivity of air is about 0.2 cm.^{2} sec.$^{-1}$. However, as in the diffusion problem, it was found that the simple theory does not fit the facts, for the only way to make the data agree with the observations is to allow the 'constant' K to increase rapidly with height. The mathematical problem then becomes much more complicated.

A satisfactory explanation of the way in which heat is transferred from the ground to the air has not yet been given. The problem is complicated because the eddies are formed not only by dynamical instability but also as a result of 'bubbles' of hot air rising from the heated surface and it is almost impossible to separate the two processes. In addition, radiation must also play a part. As a result of the study of the dynamics of heated plumes some progress has been made towards the final solution, but there is still much to be done.

At night, solar heating is absent and, with clear skies, much heat is lost from the ground by radiation. The precise determination of this loss is important economically because of the dire consequences of severe frosts to farmers and also because of the relation between ground temperatures and radiation fogs. In particular, it would be very advantageous to have a reliable formula for the prediction of night minimum temperatures.

Low night minimum temperatures are found with relatively dry air, clear skies (or only high cloud), and low winds or calms. If the air were completely dry and the sky clear, the surface would lose heat at the rate given by a well-known formula known as *Stefan's law*, which involves the fourth power of the absolute temperature of the surface. As the air is never completely dry, the radiative loss is reduced by back radiation from the water-vapour in the atmosphere near the surface. If the sky is heavily overcast, the loss is further reduced by radiation from the clouds and it is for this reason that severe frosts are unlikely in this country when there is much cloud, unless, of course, there has been an invasion of very cold air from the Arctic or from the Continent.

The radiative loss on a clear calm night depends on the temperature of the ground and on the temperature and water-vapour content of the surface air layers, which determine the back radiation. It was shown by Sir David Brunt that the back radiation can be expressed by a simple formula containing the fourth power of the absolute temperature and the square root of the vapour pressure. The temperature reached by the ground, however, depends not only on the flow of heat upwards but also on the amount of heat conducted in the ground.

By taking all these factors into account Brunt found that the temperature of the surface at any time during the night is expressed by the temperature at sunset minus a term containing the square root of the time since sunset and the thermal constants of the soil. This is known as *Brunt's parabolic formula for night minima*. When the soil constants are known accurately, the formula is reliable, but its practical application is limited by the fact that these constants change with the water content of the soil and may vary considerably from day to day. Many forecasters therefore use empirical formulae involving the dry- and wet-bulb temperatures at sunset and sometimes the wind speed, because a strong wind often prevents frost by keeping the surface air layers well mixed with warmer air from above. The 'constants' in these formulae have to be determined for each locality separately and in view of Brunt's analysis, can be regarded only as averages. As a result the formulae rarely give very accurate predictions but they have proved useful as guides.

METEOROLOGY AS AN EXACT SCIENCE

The examples given above of the application of micro-meteorology to problems which, in one way or another, affect the lives of everyone, indicate only a few of the uses of this relatively new but vigorous branch of the science of the atmosphere. The study of atmospheric diffusion, however, shows a clear difference of approach when compared with synoptic meteorology. An 'exact' science is one which admits of a quantitative approach as opposed to a purely descriptive summary of knowledge acquired by observation, and for many years meteorology languished in the latter category. Micrometeorology, from its earliest days, has had the inestimable advantage when compared with synoptic meteorology and climatology of a copious supply of really accurate observations made with sensitive instruments specially designed for the purpose. Further, the problems of micrometeorology, although undoubtedly difficult, are more easily defined in precise terms than those of synoptic meteorology, and it is thus not surprising that the mathematicians have found in the lower layers of air better opportunities than elsewhere in the atmosphere.

The difference between the two branches of the science of the atmosphere, however, goes deeper than difficulties in technique. In a micrometeorological study, say of the change in phase and amplitude of the diurnal temperature wave with height, the investigator knows in broad terms how the atmosphere will behave during the period considered – or more accurately, he studies only those periods when atmospheric conditions conform fairly closely to those postulated in his theory. If conditions change rapidly during his trials, if for example a thunderstorm breaks out during the period of observation of the propagation of the diurnal temperature wave upwards, he is as much entitled to reject the observations as irrelevant as is a laboratory physicist when a part of his apparatus burns out. The micrometeorological problem is not to predict the behaviour of the atmosphere on a certain day in the year but to make precise and quantitative the part played by certain physical processes in a well-defined situation. The end-point is not a prediction that an event will happen at a certain time, but that when conditions approach those postulated, measurement and theory will agree. Only the absence of control distinguishes an investigation of this type from its laboratory counterpart, and although the standard of accuracy is still below that of most parts of normal physics, there are good reasons for claiming that in this branch, meteorology is already an exact science.

In synoptic meteorology the philosophy is entirely different. The forecaster cannot ignore occasions when instability causes thunderstorms to form, for thunderstorms and other disturbing manifestations of convection are a part of his daily experience, not inconvenient interruptions in his work. He is paid, not to explain the weather, but to foretell it. The observations on which he has to assess a situation are few compared with the volume of the atmosphere he has to consider, but still too many to be studied in detail as the hands of the clock move relentlessly towards the hour when, come what may, he must write down his forecast.

The conclusions of the forecaster are probabilities. Like a social worker, he is aware that many facts are hidden from him and that he must call on his experience as well as his knowledge of science in deciding what is likely to happen tomorrow. Even if the mathematical approach succeeds beyond the dreams of meteorologists, it is difficult to believe that any model of the atmosphere will ever yield results comparable in precision and accuracy with, say, those of spherical astronomy. It is possible, for example (but improbable), that weather is influenced in some way by extra-terrestrial phenomena, such as bursts of cosmic radiation or meteoric showers, which themselves are unpredictable because they result from events long past, of which we cannot have any knowledge. There is no real evidence of such influences, but if the macro processes which bring about severe winters or prolonged droughts are initiated in this way, weather is genuinely indeterminate and accurate long-range forecasts are as much a dream as the philosopher's stone.

Lord Rutherford is reported to have said on one occasion that nuclear physics was a grand subject because so little was known about it. Meteorology is in much the same position. It is the most fascinating and exasperating of all the earth sciences, but one which its devotees never entirely forsake. Its history is one of many unsuccessful theories and of a few that have survived, and its path contains many twists and turns that led nowhere. Today equipped with tools of greater power than ever before, meteorology seems to be turning yet another corner and hewing for itself a better road forward. Whether or not this will be the broad highway is a forecast that no meteorologist dare make, but the signs are not unfavourable.

Meteorological Observations

THE nature of the meteorological problem requires that frequent observations be made simultaneously in the same way at many places. During the past century meteorologists have collaborated on a world-wide scale to ensure uniformity and reliability in their observations. The result is that all countries now measure the fundamental meteorological entities in precisely the same way, the only difference being in the style of their instruments.

Meteorological Stations

As an example of the organization of meteorological observations we may consider the United Kingdom. The Meteorological Office is the State Meteorological Service. It forms part of the Air Ministry (but not of the Royal Air Force) and its Director-General is responsible to the Secretary of State for Air through the Permanent Under-Secretary of State of the Air Ministry. To carry out its duties, the Meteorological Office maintains over a hundred observing and reporting stations and subsidizes a number of ancillary stations.

The observations are made for two main purposes: to enable forecasts to be prepared and to maintain a record of the climate of this country. Although there is a clear distinction between the two purposes, observations made for forecasting are also used for climatological records, but certain requirements of climatology, especially rainfall, necessitate the setting-up of more numerous but less elaborate stations. In the United Kingdom there are many stations maintained by private individuals, educational institutions, local authorities, and industrial concerns which contribute essential data to the climatological records. Very large numbers of rain gauges are maintained privately. Without such a dense network it would not be possible to assess accurately the water income of the country.

The international meteorological code approved by the World Meteorological Organization covers all the observations needed for forecasting and climatology. This is the common language of meteorologists. It has many subdivisions, especially for aviation, which need not be described in detail here. In the United Kingdom there are the following categories of stations:

(a) Full synoptic stations, staffed by professional meteorologists. Many of the stations operate on a twenty-four hour basis and are usually located on airfields.
(b) Ancillary ('AERO code') stations which make reports of weather, wind, cloud, and visibility at fixed times.
(c) Climatological stations which record certain elements at fixed hours.
(d) Health resort stations which not only act as climatological stations but make special daily reports for transmission to the Press by the Meteorological Office.
(e) Crop weather stations, maintained to assist agriculture.
(f) Research and specialized stations (e.g. for upper-air soundings and thunderstorm location).

Observations

At a full synoptic station the following observations are made at fixed observing hours:

Present weather.
Wind direction and speed.
Amount of cloud.
Form of cloud.

Height of cloud base.

Visibility.

Air temperature.

Dew point.

Barometric pressure and tendency.

Past weather (i.e. weather between the time of the previous observation and the time of the present observation).

In addition, observations are made every 3 hours on the state of the ground and of rainfall and extremes of temperature at 6 a.m. and 6 p.m. Stations which are equipped with sunshine recorders also report the number of hours of bright sunshine during the day.

Instruments

The basic equipment of a meteorological station – the barometer, thermometers, anemometer, rain-gauge, and sunshine recorder – have not changed significantly for many decades. The mercury barometer, of which the British Kew-pattern is an excellent example, is a precision instrument which supplies the synoptician with his basic data. Air temperature is measured by a sheathed mercury-in-glass thermometer kept in a louvered screen, and humidity is calculated with the aid of tables from the readings of dry-and wet-bulb thermometers kept in the same screen. Aneroid barometers and hair hygrometers are used only in the form of autographic instruments to indicate tendencies. Wind speed near the surface is measured by a pressure-tube or cup anemometer.

Instruments of this type are installed at all reporting stations. The larger stations often have much ancillary equipment, such as visibility meters and cloud-height searchlights, and research stations naturally have their own highly specialized apparatus, much of which is constructed on the spot.

The basic instruments are familiar and need not be described here. Methods of measuring the most important physical properties of the atmosphere near the ground have not changed significantly in the last fifty years; the greatest advances are those which have been made in the exploration of the upper atmosphere. The earliest measurements of pressure, temperature, and humidity high above the surface of the earth were made in manned balloons; later came kites and free balloons (*balloon-sondes*) carrying registering instruments called meteorographs, of which the Dines balloon meteorograph was an outstanding example. This instrument, which weighed only a few ounces, recorded pressure and temperature by scratches on a piece of silvered metal about the size of a postage stamp. If the instrument was found after a flight, the record could be translated into millibars and degrees with the aid of a low-power microscope.

It is obvious that this method of taking upper-air soundings suffered from several disadvantages. It was entirely a matter of chance whether the record would be found, and in any event, the details of the sounding could not be supplied in time to be of use for forecasting. These handicaps were not overcome until the radio-sonde was developed just before the Second World War.

The radio-sonde uses the method of telemetering to give information concerning the pressure, temperature, and humidity in the vicinity of a small free balloon ascending through the atmosphere. There are three main elements: the sensing devices, the transmitter, and the ground receiver. The sensing devices consist of a simple aneroid barometer, a thermometer (usually of the electrical type), and a hygrometer (usually of the hair or goldbeater skin type, although electrical devices are now being used more frequently). The transmitter is a small short-wave radio set, powered by dry batteries. Telemetering, or the transmission of information back to earth, can be done in several ways, by varying the interval between signals (chronometric sonde) by changing the pitch of an audible note, or by changing the frequency of a radio signal, all in sympathy with the changes in the properties of the air as indicated by the sensing devices. Alternatively, the indications of the sensing devices can be coded and transmitted as an ordinary message.

In the British radio-sonde, a continuous radio wave is sent out from the transmitter, modulated to a variable audio-frequency (a high-pitched whistle). As the pressure, temperature, and humidity of the air changes during the ascent of the balloon, the sensing instruments are switched into the circuit of the transmitter in turn by the action of a rotary switch. To every value of the pressure, temperature, and humidity corresponds a definite pitch, or frequency, of the audible note. At the receiving station, the pitch of the note is measured. Finally, the signals so received are converted into millibars, degrees, and vapour pressures by the use of a calibration curve prepared for the sonde before it was sent out.

When the balloon reaches a great height, usually over 60,000 feet, it bursts and the sonde falls to earth. The rate of descent is reduced by a parachute attached to the balloon. Some of the sondes are recovered (there is a small reward for their return) and are reconditioned for further use.

The radio-sonde, by making available to the forecaster up-to-date information on the properties of the high atmosphere, has brought about a great improvement in the forecasting of conditions on air routes and in our knowledge of the upper air generally. Modern sondes have reached a consistently useful standard of accuracy, but there is still room for improvement. Broadly, telemetering now presents few difficulties and the major problems are those connected with the sensing elements. The meteorological problem is very different from those of the laboratory. The instruments of the physicist are usually designed to work over a relatively small range of conditions. The barometer of the radiosonde should respond accurately to at least a ten-fold range of pressure, with the added handicap of a wide variation of temperature. The thermometer should measure the temperature of the air equally accurately in strong sunshine and in the dark wet interior of a cloud, and the hygrometer should be capable of dealing with a saturated atmosphere as well as with the extreme dryness and cold of the lower stratosphere. In addition, the instrument must be light enough to be carried by a small balloon and suitable for mass production and easy calibration. No existing sonde meets all these requirements completely satisfactorily, and research is proceeding intensively in all parts of the world to improve the accuracy and consistency of the observations. The problem is likely to become more urgent with the introduction of jet aircraft for civil operation on a global scale, for the economic operation of such aircraft depends to quite a large extent on an accurate knowledge of the temperature of the air at all levels.

Radar Wind

The old method of determining winds in the upper air depended upon the tracking of a small free balloon (pilot-balloon) by an optical theodolite. Obviously, this method could not be used when the sky was overcast, and for many years the forecaster was denied knowledge of the upper winds in a depression. If a suitable reflector is attached to a balloon, its position can be found by radar irrespective of the state of the sky. Originally, radar equipment developed for military purposes was used for this work, but in recent years special wind-finding sets have appeared on the market.

The Meteorological Office, which has eight permanent upper-air stations in the United Kingdom and seven overseas, normally makes two observations of pressure, temperature, and humidity and four observations of upper winds at each station every day. Each sonde has to be separately calibrated. Including sondes provided for some parts of the Commonwealth and for foreign customers, the Meteorological Office upper-air unit at Harrow handles over 20,000 instruments a year.

Scales of Temperature in Meteorology

IN the eighteenth century, at least 15 different scales of temperature were in use in Europe,* but by the beginning of this century only three, those of Fahrenheit, Celsius, and Réaumur had survived, with the last-named rapidly becoming obsolete. At the present time it seems likely that the Fahrenheit scale will ultimately disappear, leaving the Celsius (or Centigrade) scale in sole possession of the field.

In physics, a standard and its derived units are arbitrary. In the measurement of temperature the standard is a *fixed point*. Two fixed points were in general use in standards laboratories before 1954, namely the *ice-point,* defined as the temperature of pure ice in equilibrium with air-saturated water at a pressure of 1 atmosphere (1013·25 mb), and the *steam-point,* defined as the equilibrium temperature of pure water and steam at 1 atmosphere pressure. (In common usage, these are called the freezing point and the boiling point of water, respectively.) In 1954 it was agreed internationally to base temperature scales on one fixed point, the *triple-point* of water, the temperature at which a mixture of ice, liquid water, and water-vapour remains indefinitely in equilibrium. For brevity, this temperature is often referred to as the melting point of ice.

Standards laboratories use a number of primary and secondary fixed points for the calibration of thermometers, but for most purposes the Celsius or Centigrade scale may be regarded as determined by the readings of standard instruments capable of interpolating smoothly and reproducibly between the ice-point, which is called 0°c., and the steam-point, which is labelled 100°c. (Since 1948 there has

* As given in Parkinson's *System of Natural Philosophy* (1735)

been an international agreement among scientists to use only the word 'Celsius' for this scale, but in Britain the word 'Centigrade' is more commonly used.) The Fahrenheit scale is defined similarly, with the values 32°F. for the ice-point and 212°F. for the steam-point, so that the two degrees are related by

$$1°\text{C.} = 1\cdot8°\text{F.}$$

but, in converting from one scale to the other, allowance must be made for the change of zero. The equation for the conversion of a thermometer reading in Centigrade to its equivalent in Fahrenheit is easily memorized in the form

$$°\text{F.} = 1\cdot8°\text{C.} + 32°\text{F.}$$
$$(\text{e.g.} \quad 15°\text{C.} = (1\cdot8 \times 15 + 32)°\text{F.} = 59°\text{F.})$$

Both scales are in use in professional meteorology. The English-speaking countries use either Fahrenheit or both Fahrenheit and Centigrade, but on the continent of Europe the Centigrade scale, called Celsius, is used exclusively.

This unfortunate mixture of scales is a cause of confusion, and in 1953 the World Meteorological Organization, which controls the international meteorological codes, decided that 'degrees Celsius be used for coding temperatures in upper-air reports'. The Meteorological Office complied with this decision in 1956, and the Centigrade scale is now always used in communications to aircraft from British airports and airfields. In 1955 and 1959, the Congress of the World Meteorological Organization passed resolutions adopting in principle the Celsius degree and the metric system of units for international meteorological communications and urging all its members to conform.

In accordance with this request, the Meteorological Office gave up the use of the Fahrenheit scale in its professional work on 1 January 1961, but continued the use of that scale in public statements. In 1962 it was decided to use both scales in the general and regional forecasts. This decision followed an inquiry among the principal scientific and technical bodies and the leading makers of thermometers in Britain, all of whom were in favour of the inclusion of the Centigrade scale. At present (1963) no decision has been taken to omit the Fahrenheit scale.

Measurements and calculations in physics are invariably carried out with the Celsius (or Centigrade) degree and its associated unit, the calorie, but the Fahrenheit scale and its associated unit, the British Thermal Unit, are still used by engineers in this country. The clinical thermometer, as used by British doctors, is also graduated in degrees Fahrenheit. Meteorology is a branch of physics and should therefore use the units of the parent science, but apart from this there are good technical reasons for preferring the Centigrade to the Fahrenheit scale when describing the physical properties of the atmosphere. Near the ground, the temperature of the air fluctuates considerably, with amplitudes up to $\pm 1°$c. (approximately $\pm 2°$F.) on a sunny day; further, it varies quite considerably between places within the same forecast region. For these reasons, it is not only useless but misleading to specify atmospheric temperatures more precisely than to the nearest whole degree Centigrade except for certain special purposes, such as the determination of relative humidity by the wet-and-dry bulb method. The Centigrade scale has also the considerable advantage that it singles out the temperature at which water normally freezes by making it the dividing line between positive and negative values. A negative Centigrade temperature is highly significant in public forecasts, for it calls attention to the hazards of a freeze-up. The Fahrenheit has the unremarkable number 32 for the most important temperature in the scale, and severe frosts can occur with positive Fahrenheit temperatures. All told, there are good reasons for claiming that the Centigrade scale is especially well adapted for meteorological use.

The conversion from the Centigrade to the Fahrenheit

scale is not a particularly simple mental operation because of the change of zero and the multiplying factor 1·8. For those who use weather forecasts chiefly as a guide to comfort and outdoor activities, but are not accustomed to the Centigrade scale, the following easily memorized guide may prove useful:

0°c. and all minus values	freezing
5°c.	cold
10°c.	chilly
15°c.	mild
20°c.	warm
25°c.	hot
30°c. and above	very hot ('heat wave')

In scientific papers on meteorology, use is sometimes made of the so-called Kelvin or absolute scale of temperature. In thermodynamics it is necessary to employ a scale that does not depend upon the properties of a specific substance such as water. The Kelvin or absolute scale may be regarded, for most purposes, simply as the Centigrade scale with 273° added, so that in this system the average temperature of the air near the surface of the earth is 288°k. or 15°c. The strict definition of the triple-point of water is 273·16°k.; the value 0°k. is often referred to as the absolute zero of temperature.

Biographical Notes

Gabriel Daniel Fahrenheit (1686–1736) was a German physicist and instrument-maker who introduced the mercury thermometer in 1720 and demonstrated the dependence of the boiling point of a liquid on pressure.

Anders Celsius (1701–44) was a Swedish astronomer who introduced the 'Centigrade' scale by dividing the difference between the freezing and boiling points of water into a hundred parts, but in his original scale the boiling point was called 0° and the freezing point, 100°.

William Thomson, Lord Kelvin (1824–1907), was one of the greatest of the Victorian scientists. He made outstanding contributions to many branches of physics, especially thermodynamics and electricity.

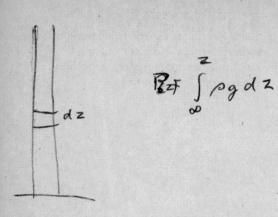

$$P_{zf} \int_{\infty}^{z} \rho g \, dz$$

Index

Index

Some Pelican books of related interest
are described
on the following pages

THE FACE OF THE EARTH

G. H. Dury

The young natural science of geomorphology – the study of the form of the ground – is much less forbidding than its name. It is developing fast, and already promises to achieve some independence both of geology and of physical geography. In this book a professional geomorphologist tells how this field of knowledge is advancing, examines some of the hotly-disputed problems which have to be solved, and discusses the processes by which construction and erosion affect the physical landscape. Among the topics receiving attention are the weakening of rocks by weathering, their removal by the forces of erosion, the cyclic development of the land-surface, the evolution of river-systems, the effects of volcanic action and of glaciers, and the surface forms of deserts.

In choosing his examples, the author has been able to select freely from the results of his own field work. There are 102 diagrams in the text and 48 pages of plates.

THE FACE OF THE SUN

H. W. Newton

A special job of astronomers during the International Geophysical Year, when this book first appeared, was the study of the surface of the sun. The tools which modern technical skill has newly placed at their service, among them radio telescopes such as that at Jodrell Bank, are adding almost daily to our knowledge of the constitution and the activity of the one star we can observe at what, in terms of stellar distances, may be called 'close range'.

Mr Newton tells the story of what men have learnt about the sun during the three and a half centuries since Galileo's early telescope first disclosed the existence of sunspots. The fifty-thousand-mile-long tongues of gas which shoot out from the sun's surface into space, the streams of solar particles which enter earth's atmosphere to cause magnetic storms that disturb our radios and to paint the night sky with displays of the Aurora Borealis, and the obscure effects of solar activity on our weather conditions are described, discussed, and so far as is yet possible explained.

And – because our sun, we may suppose, is in many ways typical of many of the countless stars of remotest space – we are given a glimpse of happenings far beyond our own system, in similar stars at the remotest bounds of the universe.

For a complete list of books available please write to Penguin Books whose address can be found on the back of the title page